THE PERGAMON ENGLISH LIBRARY

EDITORIAL DIRECTORS: GEORGE ALLEN AND BORIS FORD

EXECUTIVE EDITOR: ESMOR JONES

PUBLISHER: ROBERT MAXWELL, M.C., M.P.

POPULAR MUSIC AND THE TEACHER

POPULAR MUSIC
AND THE TEACHER

by KEITH SWANWICK

1966
THE QUEEN EAWARD
TO INDUSTRY 1966

PERGAMON PRESS

PERGAMON PRESS LTD.

OXFORD · LONDON · EDINBURGH
NEW YORK · TORONTO · SYDNEY

First Edition 1968
Copyright © 1968 KEITH SWANWICK
Library of Congress Catalog Card No. 68–26948

Printed in Great Britain by A. Wheaton & Co., Exeter

08 012862 9

CONTENTS

FOREWORD

THIS book is not intended as a guide to the various fashionable highways and by-ways of popular music: nor does it set out to dictate the every move of teachers who are confronted by classes of teenagers. The writer certainly hopes that some information and help of this sort will be found here, but also something more.

Popular music is considered in its historical, musical, cultural and social contexts. An attempt has been made to be rid of some of the misunderstandings that have surrounded this music during the last decade or so. Only after the ground has been cleared in this way does the writer presume to make suggestions and recommendations.

Naturally enough, the book is intended primarily for teachers and musicians, but it is possible that it may be of more general interest to others who are interested in, and concerned about, our social condition and the education of young people.

Whatever the degree of conviction the reader carries away, the writer can honestly say that the work and thought involved in this brief presentation of such large issues has resulted in certain changes in his own views and opinions.

INTRODUCTION

DURING the last decade or so, teachers of music in schools have become aware of the pressures being put upon adolescent boys and girls to purchase and play music very different from that connected with school. In many cases there has been a feeling that the influence of popular music is not a healthy one and that it interferes with the work teachers are trying to do. Indeed, the mass media generally have forced teachers of English, Music and Art in particular to reconsider the nature of their 'subject', and the significance of its popular manifestations. As far as music is concerned, the situation is not helped by the confusion and uncertainty as to the content and approach for children in secondary schools. Our primary schools, by and large, seem to have a pretty clear idea of where, musically speaking, they are going, but this is hardly true of the middle school range in our secondary system. It is, of course, possible to find stimulating and meaningful work going on among classes of 14-year-olds. It is possible but not easy. Popular music only aggravates an already unsatisfactory condition. For this reason it is worth paying some close attention to the background and effects of pop music since it is often easier to diagnose and treat a malady when symptoms are strong than to prescribe for a general, grumbling ache. This book is certainly not intended as a cure-all but simply examines popular music and its background and tries to show its effects on children and on the attitudes of teachers. During the course of the investigation answers are attempted to several questions. Is pop a new phenomenon, a product of this century? Does it inhibit the work of teachers in schools? What are the elements

1

of pop that cause any such interference? How can the situation be improved? Is there any real musical value in much or any pop?

Now if we are going to make comparisons and value judgements between one piece of music and another, or one sort of music and another, we must first establish what it is that we expect from a musical experience. The purpose of this Introduction is to try to indicate a possible standpoint from which to view music. In other words, the writer must attempt to find a satisfactory description of the nature of music that will serve as an aesthetic basis for the examination of various styles and pieces. The reader who prefers to get straight down to the main topic would do well to turn now to Chapter 1 and skip what follows.

In the past there have been two main and conflicting views as to the nature of any art, two answers to the question, 'Does music express emotion and if so what emotion?' The problem is seen at its sharpest in music, since among the arts music seems to be the most abstract, or 'pure'. A painting or novel often has a fairly clear 'subject', it is *about* something. So too is opera, it has plot and character. However, when we look, for example, at a Bach fugue or Stockhausen's *Gruppen* it becomes impossible to discuss it in such terms. Such 'pure' examples of music are difficult to describe in words and any emotion involved is hard to analyse. So of all the arts, music, with its wide range of possible interpretation has most often been used on one side or the other of the debate.

One side claims among its supporters Plato, who saw in each musical mode definite emotional and moral implications. The Lydian mode he found 'lascivious', and our major scale (Ionian) he found weak in character. Here then is a clear statement of the position that music expresses many different emotions, possibly including harmful feelings and attitudes. Schopenhauer, Hegel, and more recently Deryck Cooke[1] have

[1] D. Cooke, *The Language of Music*.

taken similar standpoints, which we may call 'expressive' in implication. We should find this argument easier to maintain when considering the music of Mahler or an opera than we would if Webern or a fugue were our examples. Notice too that on this view it should be possible to examine the music of a popular song and point to certain progressions as being weak, 'lascivious', or expressing an unsatisfactory emotional state.

The alternative position is that if any emotion is generated by, or expressed in music at all, it is one feeling only, an experience of 'the beautiful'. When confronted by an object of beauty we experience this feeling in the same way that we experience fear when faced by danger. The 'form' of the work is the important thing *not* emotional content. Clive Bell and Roger Fry have proclaimed this idea under the banner of 'Significant Form' and philosophers such as Alexander, Joad, Croce and Collingwood have given their versions of it. Contemporary composers have often subscribed to this sort of statement by Stravinsky: 'I consider that music is, by its very nature, powerless to *express* anything at all.' Similarly, Hindemith has stated that music 'cannot express the composer's feelings'. This argument is not so easy to state in the face of a ballet or *La Bohème* but seems safe enough if applied to the later works of Schönberg. Popular music seen in this light hardly exists at all.

Neither of these alternatives seems satisfactory as a basic theory of music. Emotion of some description attends both the making and understanding of any work of art, and it is also clear that in some way such feeling is given shape, or structured. In an attempt to get a little nearer to the truth about the nature of music modern philosophers have been asking different questions and approaching the problem from a new angle. Two concepts in particular have emerged which throw some light on the problem of the meaning of music. The most important of these is the notion of man as a 'symbol-making' animal. Briefly, this implies that we humans are able to handle the world and come to understand it through the use of devices like language, mathematical notation and so on. The important thing is that symbols can be operated, manipulated and organised to enable reasoning in the abstract and communication of ideas and feelings to take place. Animals can communicate through *signals* but seem unable to deal with reality in symbolic ways. To a dog, a finger pointing is something to be sniffed at: to a man it means 'look over there'. This difference between symbols and signals has bearing, believe it or not, on our discussion of the adolescent and popular songs. It may well transpire that a pop song may be for one person a symbol-structure with a wealth of *meaning*, whilst for another the same song may be a signal demanding a simple response in the form of dancing, shouting or hysteria.

The second notion deserving our attention is that all human understanding, whether personal, artistic or scientific, depends on *intuition*. This really means an ability to grasp the significance of relationships and must be in attendance before even the driest logical statement can be understood. Symbol-making is only possible through the fundamental human ability of intuition. It has been shown[2] that this ability to see relationships between things not logically connected is even at the root of humour. In a pun two sets of incompatible ideas meet in one word. Scientist and artist alike have often to wait for the 'flash-over' from one field of experience to another, as the phrases 'stroke of genius' and 'flash of insight' suggest. We either 'see' the joke, 'grasp' the principle, 'appreciate' the music or we do not. No amount of logical explanation will provide the experience, as anyone who has ever tried to *explain* a joke will know.

Just what is it then that is symbolised for us in music and which we understand intuitively? It is not individual sensations or emotions, nor is it just a beautiful form. It is the dynamic pattern of feeling that is presented, 'the pattern of

[2] A. Koestler, *Insight and Outlook.*

life itself, as it is felt and directly known'. It is worth quoting
Mrs. Langer in more detail here.[3]

> The tonal structures we call music bear a close logical similarity to
> the forms of human feeling . . . forms of growth and attenuation, flow-
> ing and stowing, conflict and resolution, speed and arrest, excitement
> and calm, or subtle activation and dreamy lapses—not joy or sorrow
> perhaps, but the poignancy of either and both . . . the greatness and
> brevity and eternal passing of everything vitally felt. Such is the
> pattern, or logical form of sentience; the pattern of music is that same
> form worked out in pure measured sound and silence. Music is a tonal
> analogue of emotive life.

Such a view of music not only helps us to evaluate the worth
of particular pieces but also gives us good reason for having
music on the school time-table at all. Music is not just 'expression', nor is it a piece of tonal architecture with a beautiful shape. During its performance it is alive, a form in flux,
symbolic of human feeling. It must be able to explore truthfully the areas of feeling which it structures and if it does then
we learn something of the motions of our emotions. In a real
sense we can claim that music is 'education of feeling'.

Clearly it does not matter whether the feelings involved be
large or small provided that real exploration takes place and
that such emotional movement as there is has direction, purpose and shape. To use an analogy. Imagine feeling flowing
by like a stream of water. It is doing so as you read this book.
We may give this stream something more than its vague
meanderings by cutting a deeper, straighter channel and we
may alter its pressure and level by building a dam or locks. We
may divert it, slow it down or merge it with other water-ways.
These artificial devices make us more aware of the true nature
of water. In such a way is the composer concerned with his
music. He is not working with the flowing of the stream of
consciousness alone (that would be day-dreaming) nor merely
with the construction of various formal or organisational

[3] S. K. Langer, *Feeling and Form.*

devices (that would be science), but with the pressures, tensions and flow of feelings around and through the constructional elements. In more realistic terms, we are divided creatures with complex and often powerful feelings, but also with the insight and intelligence to observe and in some measure to direct these emotions. The creative artist is one person who can unite for us instinct and intellect and explore the relationships. Form and feeling are the warp and weft of music and the arts, and a valid symbol of their relationship must be truthful on both counts.

How does all this help when it comes to examining popular music? Firstly, we shall be wary of dismissing it on the grounds that it has no great complexity. Neither has a folk-song, but there is no reason to complain of this if it shows us feeling truthfully on its small scale. Secondly, we shall be careful about criticising popular songs because they may happen to be crude, or on the surface ugly. An artist can handle in his work the movements of any part of the spectrum of human emotion, including erotic feelings, violence, treachery and ugliness as well as feelings of which we are more proud. An appreciation of Shylock or Caliban is a deepening of experience. And thirdly, we shall avoid the trap of giving to certain musical progressions, out of context, the credit for expressing either 'good' or 'harmful' emotions. The issue is more subtle than that.

CHAPTER 1

THE 'HIGH' AND THE 'LOW'

"The distinction between higher and lower musician appears
to go back to the very beginning of musical history."[1]

MARIUS SCHNEIDER

It is often assumed that popular music is something peculiar to
this century and that it has no historical precedent. The purpose of this chapter is to explore a little, to try to get pop music
into historical perspective. In doing so we may find not only
that we understand something of its musical roots, but also that
there is a good deal of historical material available which may
well be useful for the teacher. We shall notice also a permanent
kind of tension between the formal and expressive elements in
music, between the intensity and immediacy of emotion on the
one hand, and the structural factors through which feelings are
shaped and displayed on the other. 'Folk song' and 'art music'
will appear under many different names.

Primitive Music, Greeks and Romans

Most of our information about the music of primitive peoples
tends to come from observations of isolated and 'backward'
communities that can still be found in various parts of the
world. It is worth continuing the quotation at the head of the
chapter.

> In the primitive community of the Andaman Islands everyone is
> allowed to compose his own songs, but not everyone is authorized to
> recite the tribal legends. Among the peoples of central Asia the
> narrator of the tribal myths is often also a *shaman*. The priest-musician

---

[1] M. Schneider, *New Oxford History of Music*, Vol. 1, pp. 40 ff.

endowed with medical knowledge, whose songs reach the world of the gods, has a distinct role in such communities ... In Sahel and the western Sudan, society is divided into five castes: aristocrats, bondsmen, smiths, bards, and inferior musicians. The bards (*dialli*) are the custodians of lofty epic art and rank as great warriors. The inferior musicians, on the other hand, devote themselves to popular entertainment and their task in war is to goad on the mass of fighting men with their shouts and songs.

If we think about it our own set-up is much the same. We certainly have 'inferior' musicians who devote themselves to popular entertainment, and our entertainers are quite willing to keep up the morale of the troops. All the same, it is more difficult to imagine many of our poets and composers as great warriors. But here is an apparent division, between the formal musician who helps to keep the tribe together and make them conscious of their history and myths, and the pop singer concerned with less dignified subjects, less complex interactions of form and feeling. Yet in spite of this difference in function both sorts of music-making are woven out of the same material. Both 'high' and 'low' acknowledge the magical and religious qualities of their music. When a primitive man sings at his work his song 'serves both to lighten his labour and to appease the spirit of the felled tree or the gods of the water he is crossing'.

The distinction between 'high' and 'low' can be seen again through Greek and Roman writings. In Ancient Greece, alongside the epic tales of gods and heroes, the plebeian wind instruments and country dances are described.[2] In Rome, the division reveals itself between the professional and the amateur. Society considered Nero badly behaved because he played as a *professional* and not as a *gentleman* musician. The former would be paid fantastic engagement fees, they often displayed 'temperament', and their music was often a means to the end of success in competitions. The professional was the 'low' musician, whilst among the aristocracy there was a feeling that

[2] Homer, *Iliad*.

the best music belonged to the past. This respect for the ancient
is often to be found in communities that have little significant
contemporary art. The same sort of situation existed to some
extent in England during the first half of our century. Respect
for music of the past has often conflicted with modern developments and with our 'low' music. The division noted so far
between high and low; aristocratic and plebeian; amateur and
professional; old and new; can be found in some disguise or
other at any point of history. Generally speaking, it is possible
to make a distinction between music that is mainly, for want of
a better word, *formal*; well rooted in the past and serving those
areas of feeling concerned with continuity, tribal unity, and
religious world views, and the more *expressive* styles; concerned
with more immediate and transient feelings. All of these elements provide legitimate material for the musician.

The Middle and Golden Ages

In the Middle Ages the difference in emphasis is between the
music of the Church and the minstrel. The musician–magician
of the primitive community has turned monk, and as the sole
guardian of written tradition, is able to preserve simple,
austere songs that reflect continuity of tradition and the meaning of the Faith. The minstrel, by contrast, had neither the
knowledge nor the desire to function in this way.

> They appeared at court festivals and in the castles of the highest
> nobility: but they were also in evidence at the noisy feasts of the citizen
> class, at tournaments and warlike assemblies, and were not averse to
> furnishing the music for peasant weddings. They took part in the
> performance of religious plays, and their activities embraced, besides
> singing and fiddling, the recitation of legends, acrobatic stunts, and
> magic tricks.[3]

An interesting link between minstrel and Church is the
troubadour, who preserved and used church modes and sang of

[3] P. H. Lang, *Music in Western Civilisation.*

lofty sentiments, and yet sometimes asked the help of minstrels in the arrangement and even the performance of his songs.

If any period of Western music history comes really close to revealing a unity of formal and expressive qualities, it is surely the so-called Golden Age, beginning in the sixteenth century. By this time the permitted music of the Church was of a wider range, with more freedom to express and illuminate religious subjects in dramatic or sensuous ways. The style of the secular madrigal is often identical with the church motet. It is worth remembering that all Palestrina's madrigals were given alternative sacred words by admirers. Both art forms employ complex polyphony and expressive vocal line and harmony. Pattern and pressure of feeling seem equally strong. There is, of course, music connected with the illiterate and rural community, which has none of the complexity of madrigal or motet. And yet, the 'high' musician was able to take the 'low' folk-tune and use it in composition. John Bull's keyboard piece, *Walsingham*, is an example. As the simple tunes of rural England permeated upward, so did the contrapuntal devices filter down to the tavern, in the form of round or catch. It is true that the simple and sometimes crude counterpoint involved bears little comparison with the finely wrought work of Gibbons, Byrd, or Morley: yet at least the contrapuntal principle was understood by the artisan. Likewise the lute songs of John Dowland, following the old minstrel tradition, were popular right through society.

It is too easy to paint a false and idealistic picture of the situation at this time, but it is certain that musical divisions were not quite so evident as in other periods. It should be noted, however, that most of written or printed music was complex, whereas, as far as we can tell, the unwritten songs were simple enough to be remembered and passed along in aural tradition. It is no accident that Byrd, for one, should have been fascinated by the prospect of getting music into print. The division is no longer between religious and secular, but between the music of literate and illiterate communities. From this point our 'high' and 'low' musicians come into sharper relief.

Baroque and Opera

During that movement in the seventeenth century known as 'Baroque', we find a swing away from the complex constructions of the previous era. 'The man of the baroque loves unrest and tension and the overwhelmingly pathetic. The baroque artist frowns upon strict form and harmony of proportions as being too doctrinal and coercive.'[4] Generally speaking, music becomes simpler in texture and brighter in sound. Dance rhythms become prevalent, and the bar-line comes into power as a unit of accent and pulsating motion. The new, bright-sounding violin begins to replace the more sombre tones of the viol; the orchestra is used in contrasting sections of colour, and the trumpet displayed in sparkling, stirring ways. The aesthetic notion of the age was that of the 'affections', and great emphasis was placed on the *physical* effects of sound. The Saxon court conductor, Heinichen (1683–1729), attacked the conservatives for their 'exaggerated metaphysical contemplations' and proclaimed that the only thing that mattered should be 'how the music sounds and how the listeners like it'. This argument has been used much more recently than in the seventeenth century. It sounds rather like something from *Juke Box Jury*. In broad terms, this was a period of expressive devices, novelties, striking effects and bright sounds which appealed to a wide range of taste, popular and aristocratic. The airs of Lully in France, and Handel in England found their way into the carols and culture of the poorer sections of society, and a little later, folk-tunes would be heard in the opera house.

It is worth noting a sort of split occurring in opera after about 1700. The florid solo line of high opera and the conventions of

---

[4] Lang, *op. cit.*

plot and manner that had evolved and hardened since 1600 were not enjoyed or supported by everyone. *The Beggar's Opera*, by John Gay, first performed in 1728, was a successful attempt to remedy matters. With its street-corner characters and borrowed popular tunes it soon gained international repute. Many of the songs were folk-tunes but some were borrowed wholesale from Handel. This strange mixture of music shows the 'high' and the 'low' in communication with each other. However, as 'serious' opera became more and more set in its ways, rigid and stylized, confining its attention to lofty and tragic subjects, the desire for 'light relief' created a brand-new medium. Lighter fare was introduced in the form of entertainment in the intervals, under the name 'Intermezzo', or 'Intermède'. Rousseau[5] defined the latter thus:

> A piece of music or dance inserted at the Opéra or sometimes at the Comédie between the acts of a big piece, to cheer and repose in some measure the spirit of the spectator, saddened by thoughts of the tragic and strained by its attention to matters of gravity.

He only objects to this practice if the centre of interest happens to be different, 'tossing and tugging the attention of the spectator, as one might put it, in a contrary direction'. In time, this lighter part grew longer and was eventually established as a form in its own right—*opéra buffa*. Early examples of *opéra buffa*, such as *La Serva Padrona*, by Pergolese, were entitled 'Intermezzo'. *Opéra comique* is rather different, and was first presented in 1715 at the Paris fair of St. Germain. It set out to imitate and parody grand opera. The spoken word carries the plot along with songs now and then. This is where we find some of the roots of modern musical comedy and the satirical show, and it is of interest to note that the term 'vaudeville' originally meant a Paris street-song of a satirical nature.

So far we have seen the 'high' and 'low' musician operating in different ways. Sometimes it is not easy to apply these rough labels, but, in general, the former consolidates and con-

[5] Quoted by Scholes, *Oxford Companion to Music*.

serves by providing complex symbol-structures which articulate in some detail the 'place' of man in society and among the gods, while the latter is busy with the simpler responses of man to his immediate surroundings. To some extent, as we have seen, the 'low' has relied upon the 'high' for devices of technique, for patronage and privilege. The minstrel was employed by the Church and the gentry; the counterpoint of the sixteenth century was echoed to some degree in the taverns; tunes by Lully found their way into the street, and light opera began in the house of *opéra seria*. Now to some extent this interaction can be traced into this century of ours, but the most disturbing fact at present is the lack of communication between the 'classical' and 'popular' worlds. The division is no longer between magic and work, religious and secular, urban and rural, literate and uneducated. It is certainly not between professional and amateur. The seeds of our divisions are found in Vienna between the years 1750 and 1830. Here, the philosophy of Leibniz, assuming that truth should be sought by reason alone, permeates the work of artist and musician. It is here that the thin edge of the wedge is inserted into the musical life of society.

Classical and After

Remind yourself of the sound of early Haydn and Mozart. Here is popular music, light, entertaining, witty and graceful. It is almost ironic that the cheerful, open-air serenades of this time should, through a process of evolution, be changed in name and mood into the medium of the string quartet. It may have something to do with the increasing skill of string players between the early divertimenti and the last quartets of Beethoven, but the overriding factor is surely the social and political atmosphere of the time. The conflict of mind and feeling between the older, aristocratic, reactionary forces and revolutionary ideals is present even in the music of Haydn's middle years. The earlier style of writing, with movements organised about one key centre and proceeding logically and gracefully through related keys, gives way to conflict of themes and keys, with sudden interruptions and a great deal of stormy development in the centre of movements. The apparently happy Haydn, who spent most of his working life in the service of Prince Esterhazy, had certain feelings about 'class' that have not often been noted.[6] 'I have had converse with emperors, kings, and many great lords, and I have heard many flattering praises from them; but I do not wish to live on a familiar footing with such persons, and I prefer people of my own class.' Later in life he was happy to step outside of the system of patronage. The younger Mozart quarrelled with his patron, the Archbishop of Salzburg, and ended his life in poverty, a result, to some extent, of this action. In terms of music it was Beethoven, of course, who brought things to a head with his stormy and heroic symphonies, particularly the 'Seventh'.

> For this titanic assertion of the Ego heralds the death-throes of the autocracies of the seventeenth and eighteenth centuries as surely as the birth of opera in the seventeenth century had meant the end of such vestiges as survived the Middle Ages.[7]

But while Beethoven proclaimed revolution, and in his later years a mystical acceptance of life, the 'public' went another way. His uncompromising creations were, in the course of time, put aside in favour of those who quite deliberately set out to entertain. The Augarten concerts in Vienna, when first dedicated to the public by Emperor Joseph II, presented programmes which included a good deal of Mozart and Beethoven. Gradually, these names all but disappeared and the lighter music of Pamer, Lanner, and the Strausses became popular. How many people today, when the music of Vienna is mentioned, think of Haydn, Mozart, Beethoven and

[6] Wilfred Mellers, *Music In The Making*.
[7] Mellers, *op. cit.*

Schubert? It is as if society had accepted Dr. Burney's view of music, when he called it 'an Innocent Luxury, unnecessary indeed to our Existence', with the result that the 'high' musician can find no place in the community for music of any great weight and formal significance. As a result he sets his face *against* society, no longer serving it, but denouncing it.

> We can see the beginning of this attitude in Beethoven, for although Beethoven was outwardly a successful man and a national, even a European hero, yet he was unsuccessful in that he was not revered for his greatest music—as Byrd and Lully and Couperin and even Haydn certainly had been. In composing pieces like *The Battle of Vittoria* Beethoven must have been the first composer to write bad music for a public that he despised.[8]

Apart from the personal character of Beethoven there were two allied developments that increased the distance between the lighter and more substantial kinds of music. Due to the growth in size of the orchestra, and due to the demands of a larger proportion of the community for music, the old venue of court and home gave way to newly built concert halls. Two things resulted. In the first place, the composer could no longer direct or take part in every performance of his work, as was the case with Bach and even Haydn, and secondly, a real physical gap was carved between performer and audience. Instead of the music being presented in the intimate atmosphere of the drawing-room, on the same level and surrounded by the listeners, the work had to be projected over the edge of a platform to fill a large area of space.

To satisfy the more varied tastes of a large and very mixed gathering, the programme and the attitude of the performer came to be modified. The net result was to encourage a class of performer who was prepared to travel from hall to hall, city to city, and so build up a reputation by entertaining, in one way or another. Music had become in our modern sense a commodity. The performers may have been free from the limiting demands of one rich patron, but they often had to resort to all

[8] Mellers, *op. cit.*

sorts of tricks to secure engagements. The new 'grand' piano, with a steel frame to enable it to withstand violent punishment, came into its own and in the early days Liszt produced and played the noisy, dazzling pieces that were so popular. We might notice that women were said to be most affected by his appearance, especially the long hair! The day of the virtuoso had begun. Players like Paganini imitated the sounds of animals on their instruments, or played blindfold, or played with only two or three strings on their instrument. Concert programmes between the beginning and the middle of the nineteenth century changed out of all recognition. At Beethoven's own concert in 1808, the programme included his Fifth and Sixth symphonies, the Choral Fantasia, part of the Mass in C, and the G Major Piano Concerto. The composer also improvised on the piano. By the middle of the century it was rare to hear a whole symphony, and when you did there would be certain embellishments. 'Paganini would give a concert for the background of which he would select a Beethoven symphony, performing between the movements his own breathtaking glissandos, harmonics, and double-stops.'[9]

The split between the so-called 'serious' composer and the public, ever widening during the nineteenth century, is found in a most telling way in Schumann. Here was a composer, introspective and sensitive, who carried on writing music that was to mean little in terms of financial success, while his wife toured Europe, often giving displays on the piano similar to those in which Paganini delighted. In this way they managed to live. Schumann has been called a 'children's composer', a 'domestic' musician, and his pieces are intended, by the nature of their careful counterpoint and subtle dynamics, for performance on the small, household upright piano, not on the concert 'grand'. In other words, he avoids the medium in which his wife was so successful. From his day to ours there have been artists who, rejecting the demands of the public for

[9] Lang, *op. cit.*, p. 968.

entertainment, have retreated into a small, enclosed area of their art. Instead of working as a sort of craftsman in the world and in society, they have often developed a style which is a closed book for all but a few devotees. Of course, people have always demanded entertainment.

What is different about our situation compared with that before the nineteenth century is that the basic vocabulary of 'serious' composers is not the same as that of the purveyor of 'light' music, and also, those who prefer to be entertained without effort now have the purchasing power to pay the piper and call the tune. Mozart could write to be profound or entertaining but after Beethoven the composer has to decide in which field he will be a specialist. We have seen certain connections between high and low in the past; an interaction between composer and folk-singer, the Church and the minstrel, serious and comic opera, the serenade and string quartet. This is to be expected and indeed, such interrelation is vital if the composer is to communicate through his work with other people. If composers ignore the simpler means of music-making and retreat, under pressure, from society into private worlds then, ultimately, they cease to be understood. We have at present an extreme example of this position in the person of Kaikhosru Sorabji, who has not only produced difficult and complex music but has forbidden its performance, on the grounds that neither performers nor listeners are yet developed enough to understand it. When this happens, the community finds other musicians both willing and able to perform the service of writing for society at large, and usually gives an ample financial reward. Those who are not interested in the huge egoistic world-view of Wagner, or who cannot understand the references to the past in Sibelius and Vaughan Williams, or the torturous nature of much modern music, have turned elsewhere for satisfaction. From the earlier English concert tradition of dining to music evolves the nineteenth-century music hall, with its showy chairman and often freakish turns.

Taking their cue from the dance tunes of Chopin and Brahms the waltz specialists come forward. Instead of uninterrupted symphonies the virtuosi hold the stage. Out of *opéra seria* grows *opéra buffa*, and later, operetta. Spontini, Rossini, Meyerbeer, Gounod, Offenbach, Strauss, Gilbert and Sullivan, musical comedy, the music hall and variety: these, it has been said, form an unbroken line to the juke-box.[10] But one important element is missing from this progression.

Music from America

The music with which we have been concerned so far derives mainly from Germany, Austria, France and Italy, with a shining contribution from England about 400 years ago. By the turn of this century the influence of the New World begins to be felt. The evolution of the 'serious' composer in America has been well described elsewhere,[11] but it is the strange amalgam of the more popular music that demands our attention.

To begin with it was imported songs, such as *Auld Lang Syne* and *Home Sweet Home*, that were the most well known during the early nineteenth century. But in the 1830's, Thomas 'Daddy' Rice created the character 'Jim Crow', a down-and-out Negro, and so began the coon, minstrel era which lasted in full flush, at any rate until the First World War. Stephen Foster began his career in the 1840's with songs like *Oh Susanna*, *Swanee River* and *Jeanie with the Light Brown Hair*. This was at the same time that *The Bohemian Girl* by Balfe was introduced, and, incidentally, that Mendelssohn was writing some of his music for *A Midsummer Night's Dream*. In the 1860's there were stirring tunes for the Civil War and in the 1870's the real negro spiritual became more widely known. At this time Sullivan made his American debut with *The Lost Chord* and

[10] W. Dunwell, *Music and the European Mind*, London: Jenkins, 1962, p. 192.
[11] Mellers, *Music in a New Found Land*, London: Barrie & Rockliff, 1964.

Wagner composed a bad march for the Philadelphia Centennial. Towards the end of the last century the favourites were Sullivan, Johann Strauss (*Die Fledermaus*) and John Philip Sousa with military music, such as *The Washington Post March*. The great era of dancing began after 1910, the Foxtrot being one surviver from a number of 'animal' dances, and nearly every song was arranged at some time or other into strict tempo. America had social troubles during the 'twenties', a 'rowdy, bawdy, unashamed orgy of irresponsibility',[12] in which jazz, with its strong down-town and sexual implications flourished.[13] Off-beat rhythms began to permeate everywhere. *Rhapsody in Blue* by Gershwin was a very early attempt to fuse jazz with the older European styles. (It was first played in 1924.) Later, Cole Porter became successful with songs like *Don't Fence Me In*. In the 1940's Richard Rodgers launched *Oklahoma*.

Dr. Spaeth makes no attempt to whitewash Tin Pan Alley,[14] but he does see vitality in some of America's popular offerings, especially when serious music

> of the so called 'classical type' still flounders about in imitation of European models, showing few if any national characteristics and no connection whatever with contemporary human experience. There is encouragement, however, in the thought that America's learned composers in the larger forms are gradually becoming aware of their shortcomings, perhaps even trying to reach an audience beyond their own little group of serious experimentalists, while our 'popular' music, in the hands of increasingly well-trained creators, has through the years gained steadily in dignity, technical solidarity and artistic significance, without losing any of its general appeal.

This sort of statement would need some qualification before it could be accepted by most 'serious' musicians, but it does indicate clearly the need of our times, the desire for the 'low' musician *reflecting* the age, the longing for simplicity. No generation is without its own variety of folk-music.

[12] S. Spaeth, *A History of Popular Music in America*.
[13] Jazz is discussed in some detail in the next chapter.
[14] Spaeth, *op. cit.*, p. 581.

Summary and Conclusions

It would be as well to summarise the main points of this chapter, since it is very compressed and rather complicated. We have postulated the existence of a 'high' and 'low' musician from time immemorial. The function of the former has been to recite the tribal lays, to unify and consolidate the community and to display religious or philosophical feelings. He deals with the lofty emotions and gives them shape in sound. The latter, on the other hand, uses music to lighten his labour, to stir up feelings in battle and to sing of comedy and love and lesser issues. His province is the surface feeling, the immediate, and those strong drives for release from boredom or anxiety. Both have a part to play. At various times the 'high' has patronised the 'low' and the expressive musician, in turn, has stimulated those whose music was formally more elaborate. But eventually, the world of opera was divided into serious and comic, the serenade evolved into the string quartet leaving nothing quite like it in its place, the symphony was set against the waltz, and the heroic concerto was deserted in favour of the virtuoso clown. Our own century demonstrates classical set against popular, the ivory tower as a refuge from 'mass culture', the formal patternings of the high-brow unintelligible to all but a few, and the popular song rejected by musicians and teachers because it seems to express 'bad' or 'diluted' feelings, without sense or shape.

To revert to the analogy of the stream, we may say that, on the one hand, we have the various artificial structures and devices but without any water, without any pressure and flow of feeling. On the other hand, popular music often seems to be a haphazard torrent of mixed and confused emotion, pouring down without any interaction with the intellect. Either extreme is worth very little as music. There is no reason why the two elements of feeling and form should not still coexist, since after all, they provide the polarity of the artist's work. What is wrong with the present situation is that there is little or no communication between the two camps. The rise of 'democracy' has forced the gap wider than it has ever been before. Democracy, plus a growing system of communications, has meant the fall of the old patrons and a spreading out of patronage over the whole community. In these matters we still tend to think in terms of the happiness of the greatest number, and the greatest number are not always the most discriminating. We can see it at work in one of our patronising institutions, the B.B.C. The B.B.C., when it was formed in 1922, took over quite a slice of the role of patron in something of the older style. In 1946 it saw fit to introduce the 'Third' programme, not because of popular demand, but because of respect for a minority who would use it and a desire to establish standards. Since then, we have been in the interesting position of observing reaction to 'pirate' radio, which, we are told, came into being as a response to demand. What could be more democratic? Be this as it may, in 1967 the forcible closure of such radio stations was followed by the opening of 'Radio One', which took over to some extent both the role, the style and the personnel of the pirate programmes. Here demand has filtered upwards from the many to the few. Our radios do not play what was decreed by the Esterhazy family, but that which gives satisfaction to Bill Smith and Jill Brown.[15] In reaction to this, some of our composers seem to be making themselves deliberately obscure.

We can now state that popular music itself, derived from and relating to more simple everyday experience, is by no means a new phenomenon, a mere product of this half-century. What is new is the specialisation that is evident in the writing of the various sorts of music and the almost complete divorce of 'high' from 'low'. The reasons for this are social and political and have to do with improved communications in the Western

[15] No criticism of any sort is implied in this paragraph and the issues which it raises are given some attention in later chapters.

world. The fact that a popular music exists need not distress those who work with music among our children. The teacher should only become concerned if he finds that his outlook and attitudes are in opposition to those of his pupils, and this, so many believe, is the case at present. Our task now is to examine jazz, from which we can learn much about pop music, and to investigate the musical and cultural significance of such music. Only then can we begin to pick up the pieces and make positive suggestions.

CHAPTER 2

JAZZ

"There has always been a temptation in language to treat the
social, the historical, and the moral scale as equivalent: to group
the ancient with the noble and the restrained, and the modern
with the vulgar and the indulgent. Luckily this tendency was
sometimes counteracted by those who equated the plain and
humble with the good, and the ornate with the stilted, affected,
and degenerate."[1]   E. H. GOMBRICH

WE HAVE briefly looked at several elements of popular music
in the past; notably minstrels, comic opera, dance tunes from
Vienna, and the very mixed and often imported music in
America. Of all the music evolved and developed in this con-
tinent, jazz is by far the most important to our theme. Here we
shall find a good deal that is basic to popular music, some
interesting classroom material and a fair amount of food for
thought. There are many differing views as to what jazz is all
about, especially among those who play it, but most people are
agreed as to its origins and it is to these that we first turn.

Origins

The basic musical culture that eventually became known as
'jazz' can be traced without doubt to the Negro section of the
American population, to the descendants of slaves transported
from their native Africa at the time of the 'Golden Age' of
English music. There is enough evidence on record to show
that, during the years of slavery, these transported Africans
were badly treated. Obviously they had little opportunity to

[1] E. H. Gombrich, *Art and Illusion.*

understand and enjoy the finer points of European art music. There was, of course, the inevitable folk-song element in their lives, and this can be divided into three rough categories. There were love-songs, though often near to irony, later called 'blues'. There were work-songs to assist with monotonous and heavy labour, such as the laying of railway track, and there were religious songs. The latter—the spiritual—originated from the Presbyterian 'Camp Meeting' at the beginning of the last century. They tend to be either Negro versions of bible stories (*Go Down Moses*) or anticipation of a better existence after death. ('Oh when I get to heaven I'll walk all about; there's nobody there for to turn me out.') The essential difference to be seen between the music in the older, European tradition and this music is in the emphasis on certain basic musical elements.

European music had demonstrated first *melody* and later, from the Middle Ages, *harmony*. African music and the music of the East take hold of *rhythm* and *timbre* to a much greater extent. In this way, the musical language reflects the spoken language.

> Their drum language was not, as is generally believed, a kind of primitive Morse code, but was a mechanical reproduction of their own vocal language, achieved by different pressures of the drum head, whilst the more subtle vibrato or 'shaking' effects were produced by knee vibration against the drum. In this way it was, and still is, a method of talking phonetically on drums, and the term 'Speaking Drums' is an exact description.[2]

The full meaning of speech amongst Africans depends to a large extent on the quality of the sound and on its rhythmic organisation. It is these elements, so important in speech, that became central to the musical style we now know as jazz.

After the Civil War and the 'liberation' in 1865, Spanish and French popular music was incorporated to some extent into the musical vocabulary of the Negro communities. The limited resources and the crowded and mixed living conditions made absorption of foreign influences inevitable. The armies

[2] Rex Harris, *Jazz*, p. 17.

of the Civil War provided a source of disused musical instruments which were taken over, in one way or another, by Negro groups. This explains in part why the military instruments, the 'blown' and portable instruments, were, and still are, most favoured by jazz musicians. With such instruments the negro extended his own singing voice. The man who blew down a trumpet was not trying to make a sound like that of European brass players but to amplify and intensify the out-of-tune, coarse, scooping, blues-singing voice. Because of this fresh start with old instruments the range of timbre has been stretched, just as, in another direction, jazz has enlarged and extended our rhythmical vocabulary.

The history of jazz from the second decade of this century becomes both confused and controversial. Various schools and styles sprang up around individuals such as 'King' Oliver and Dodds in Chicago, Beiderbecke in 'white' Chicago and many others. Other influences such as the piano Rag (French origins) and broad styles like Boogie Woogie, Swing, Sweet, Bop, Dixie, Jam and Progressive show something of the diversity of the jazz experience. To simplify matters somewhat we can distinguish three main categories amongst contemporary jazz musicians. You can be 'mainstream' and play improvised music sounding something like 1920's jazz (the 'Golden Age' of jazz), or you can be more commercial and find a style of playing that attracts audiences (the music of the dance hall and the pop-music record chart and the large 'swing' band), or you can become more refined and subtle and play in one of the idioms labelled 'modern'. This rather rough grouping would cut across some of the ideas jazz men tend to have about their work, and some of them seem to drift in and out of such categories. However, it is a useful working definition. The names of Armstrong and Barber may be taken to represent the first group, Glen Miller and Acker Bilk (swing and pseudo-Dixie) the second, and Brubeck and the Modern Jazz Quartet the more experimental kind of player.

Any reader who is well informed about jazz will be able to recognise the extent to which this account so far has been simplified. However, since it is the purpose in this chapter to explore the fundamentals of jazz experience and not jazz history, it is hoped that the writer may be forgiven two further generalisations. Firstly, a good deal of the difference between one style and another is about the relative strength of the 'beat': the further away a 'combo' (combination of instruments) strays from a heavy, regular four-in-a-bar, the more 'modern' it becomes, and the less likely to have wide popularity. Secondly, as a working definition of jazz with its many facets and developments, we can say that it is not so much a kind of music as a way of playing whatever happens to be available; the negro way.

Attitudes

Reactions to and opinions about jazz are varied and interesting. Spaeth[3] sets the 'Golden Age' of jazz alongside the social climate.

> We consumed quantities of bad liquor, sat around in speakeasies or danced like animated sardines on crowded floors. Women began to smoke, drink and tell shady stories in public, and 'flaming youth', represented by the 'flapper', the 'gigolo' and the 'cake-eater', went in for sex without inhibitions.
>
> Jazz was the inevitable music of such an unrestrained society. Its own background of dives, brothels and savagery made it an ideal expression of complete freedom from convention, and its distortions of musical tradition accurately fitted the same spirit in human behaviour.

This interesting opinion, from one who believes in the value of popular music, will be considered later. Certainly jazz was, at first, if not now, sensual and erotic in character. The implications of such common terms as 'bump', 'grind', 'black bottom', and even 'swing' and 'jazz' itself cannot be overlooked. All the same, we can see in jazz the expressive and down to earth features of folk-music. The 'music of the people'

[3] Spaeth, *op. cit.*, pp. 423–4.

is rarely delicate or refined, unless viewed through a deceiving historical haze.

Classical musicians (for want of a better term) often take the view that the best jazz players are musicians of a high order and that those who listen to jazz are often discriminating and critical. Many of our orchestral brass players have a healthy respect for the technical achievement of the jazz men, and there can be no doubt at all that these people have extended the range of tone and sound on instruments that once had very limited passages to play. Certain jazz devices have found their way into other musical styles of this century. Mutes, vibrato, flutter-tonguing and glissandi have become common property. Composers including Stravinsky,[4] Ravel, Honegger, Copland and Lambert[5] have used what amounts to a 'swung' idiom at times. However, it is possible to see this use of jazz in the same light as the use of old folk-tunes; it evokes atmosphere and provides a certain type of musical flavour with strong associations. Quite often one section of a longer work will have jazz effects which are contrasted with the remaining movements.[6] This grafting of jazz on to classical music is not often very successful, and it is doubtful whether the full potential of jazz can be realised in this sort of way. It is possible though to see such a fusion as new blood to revive 'the exhausted body of Romantic music'.[7]

The ardent jazz lover holds a much more aggressive brief and from time to time predictions are made that jazz will eventually *absorb* classical music.[8] Mr. Pleasants considers the obvious lack of communication between composer and public and sees as a solution jazz, stretching from the M.J.Q.[9] to 'Rock 'n Roll', or whatever popular music offers at any particular time. Jazz, on this view, is the great unifier; from the top to

---

[4] *Marche Royale* from *The Soldier's Tale* is an intriguing example.
[5] *The Rio Grande* has been performed effectively in schools.
[6] Ravel's Sonata for violin and piano has a blues as the second movement.
[7] Curt Sachs, *Rhythm and Tempo.*
[8] H. Pleasants, *Death of a Music.*
[9] Modern Jazz Quartet.

the bottom the basic language is the same. Now *if* this is true it carries a great deal of significance for the teacher of music in schools, for it means that if children prefer popular songs they are much nearer to the reality of the music of the future than the teacher, if he likes neither jazz nor pop music. An acceptance of this view of musical development would mean a great deal of soul-searching and this is why we have paid so much attention so far to the historical background behind our present musical set-up. Children at school are the adults of the future and if the music of the future is going to be bound up, as Mr. Pleasants suggests, with jazz, then it is time that serious consideration was made of material and methods used in our music rooms.

A superficial look at jazz and pop music will do little towards holding a clear and reasonable picture of what we should be doing in schools. It is necessary therefore to examine more closely the credentials of jazz to see whether or not it is really so vital to our times and, since a good deal of popular music is jazz-derived, to have a basis from which we can, later on, look at pop. There is another reason for such an examination; namely that jazz in its early days met with the same kind of reaction from serious musicians and people concerned with the moral welfare of the young as popular music during the last decade. Since that time jazz has become more respectable, and it provides an opportunity to look with more detachment on a social and musical phenomenon that puzzles and sometimes distresses older people. One way or another jazz is important to anyone concerned about popular music and musical standards. What does it really mean? Has it really the qualities and characteristics of folk-song?

Improvisation

It is incontrovertible that jazz, in its early days at least, was a way of singing and playing without written notation. Early work-songs, blues and spirituals, correspond in subject-matter, length, and simplicity of expression to folk-songs anywhere. A good many musical ideas were borrowed, it is true, from European popular styles and American military band and hymn-tune music, but this kind of influence is often present in folk material, as we have seen in the time of Lully and Handel. In any case such borrowings are effected aurally.

The grass roots lie in the illiterate Negro singer who sang without reference to the more complex European tradition, directly from his feelings. He sang without harmony, save that of the crudest sort, and when he eventually played an instrument he improvised around and decorated well-known songs. Depending on the work in hand, or the fancy of the moment, a note might be approached with a scoop, it might be sung flat or sharp, shouted or moaned. It is easy to take this sort of liberty when there is no printed symbol in sight. When instrumental groups were formed, reaching a musical peak in the 1920's, rehearsal was a matter of playing through old tunes repeatedly until a satisfying ensemble was reached. The simplest metric time units of two and four in a bar were adopted, and handfuls of chords familiar from march or hymn were the stock-in-trade of the pianist. On paper many jazz pieces look quite 'classical' and very tame. See how the harmonic progressions of *Doctor Jazz* compare with the Victorian hymn-tune (Example 1). In particular compare A with *a* and B with *b*, either by harmonic analysis or just the sound of each. Basically the progressions are the same. (The hymns have been transposed for easier comparison.)

The notation of jazz is only part of the story, for, in a much greater measure than in the older classical music, the thing only comes alive in performance. The harmonies, the tunes, the instruments, even the written rhythms may be commonplace, but the sound is in no way comparable to any other music. Even if a jazz score exists, it is so approximate in terms of rhythm, inflexion and tone quality as to be useful only to those who know the aural tradition. In these matters at least, improvisation is at the very core of jazz.

Example 1

(Melrose and "King" Oliver, 1927)

From St. Agnes (J. Langran 1835-1909)

From Lasus (H.A. Mann, 1850-1930)

This will be obvious to anyone who tries to reproduce from a jazz score the piece he has heard. The most 'modern' and 'intellectual' performers still stress improvisation as the mainstay of jazz activity. Even in the diluted jazz numbers that turn up in the library of large swing or stage bands,[10] or in the dance band repertory, there is still a little latitude in performance. Sometimes, in pieces written out for these bands, a shorthand way of indicating the chord sequence is used, telling the 'lead' player what is happening around him but leaving

[10] The term 'swing' in this context is used to describe the big-band style of playing which originated in the 1930's.

him some scope for improvisation. In another way such freedom from print can be seen when a whole section, say, four trumpets, will change the rhythm slightly from that indicated to obtain the effect that 'swings'. This can take place even when the particular pieces are new to the band, when they are sight-reading, thus showing the great attention paid aurally to the style of similar, known pieces. Certainly any player who prides himself on his jazz playing would place improvisation to some degree or other high on his list of required skills.

The Sound

Two things impress an outsider invited to play with a group making some kind of jazz music. One of these is the close attention paid to the tempo, to finding the 'right' speed for the basic beat; the other is the perfectionist approach to the tonal qualities of the group. If, in a large swing band for example, there are parts for four trombones then four players must be found, even if the meeting is labelled a rehearsal. The rhythm, the tunes and the harmonies will still come through with only three players but the *sound*, the timbre, is wrong. The local amateur symphony orchestra may tolerate a bassoon playing second-horn cues but this state of affairs just will not do in fair-sized jazz groups. The company must be complete, the correct types of mute inserted and a myriad ways of attack and release of notes employed. Slight acoustical differences between one room and another can take the edge off the music for the players. It is a common experience amongst jazz players that the quality of sound produced will stimulate to a high degree the standard of performance. Drummers in particular have described how a single tap on cymbal or snare-drum sets the process going. Patterns and noises emerge, and ultimately become part of a huge chain-reaction, a kind of sound orgy. The beat and the sound work upon the feelings of the musician and he responds with sounds charged with feeling. It is the reaction to the here-and-now that matters in jazz. In this way the player today is nearer in spirit to the primitive folk-singer than is the composer who uses the associations of modal progressions or folk-song arrangements as part of his larger musical design.

The Beat

Mr. Pleasants[11] asks us to imagine a 'serious' pianist and a jazz pianist sitting down to play the same jazz piece from a printed copy. To establish some degree of control over the experiment the jazz man is instructed not to improvise or depart in any way from the printed instructions. In other words his hands are tied. Yet the jazz musician will still make the piece feel like jazz whilst the other person almost certainly will not. Part of the difference is the touch of the piano, the use of the right-hand pedal and so on, but at least the basic tone will be the same for both, whereas if the instrument were a clarinet the difference would be startling. The secret, says Pleasants, is discovered when we watch the performers. The jazz man will beat time with his foot, the person not versed in jazz will not. This pulse becomes a physical action for the jazz musician whereas the other player might well think it crude or rudimentary.

> The jazz musician's view is quite another. To him the explicit beat is what sends him aloft and keeps him there. It supports his rhythmic, melodic and harmonic flight. He can be with it, ahead of it, behind it or against it; as long as his relationship to it is secure, easy and relaxed, he is, so to speak, musically airborne.

We must return to this later, but for the moment we will merely notice that a high proportion of the players in any group will be engaged in providing this essential impetus. Instruments like the bass, guitar and piano function mainly in this way as well as the more obvious percussion outfits.

We are reminded by this insistence on a dancing pulse, the

[11] *Death of a Music*, pp. 148–50.

variety of tonal resources and the measure of improvisation, of the Baroque period. 'How the music sounds and how the listeners like it', could easily be the motto in parts of the jazz world, as it was for the moderns in the seventeenth century.

Rhythm

'Rhythm is the setting-up of new tensions by the resolution of former ones.'[12] This splendid definition applies not only to musical experience but also to such physical functions as breathing and heartbeat. The pattern of changes that must occur to give our bodies some sort of permanence is reflected in the working of the mind, for as an old mental pattern blurs over, a new one is built in the same process. Anything that prepares a future is creating rhythm: ocean waves, thunder, the seasons, night and day and work itself. We even tend to organise inorganic phenomena into pulse patterns; we 'pair' the ticks of a clock into weak and strong, and the noise of wheels on the railway track is notorious for its rhythmic potential.

It is possible to describe the actual physical effects of regular sounds or light-flashes, in particular the tendency to produce hypnotic states. Rhythmic percussive noises and flashing bright lights can produce quite abnormal behaviour in the brain.

> Some people can be persuaded to dance in time with such rhythms until they collapse in exhaustion. Furthermore, it is easier to disorganise the normal function of the brain by attacking it with several strong rhythms played in different tempos.[13]

A trance-like state is often noted among primitive peoples during dancing and drumming and in more 'civilised' communities at times when music is used to induce response to religious or patriotic stimulation. This type of trance, 'being sent', can often be found where jazz or popular music is played among its fervent fans.

[12] Langer, *Feeling and Form*.
[13] W. Sargant, *Battle for the Mind*, p. 92.

Here at any rate is one element or effect of jazz which has received scientific attention. Such crude measures of response to music can be applied to some classical pieces too. The final movement of Beethoven's Seventh Symphony is often cited as an example of orgiastic dance, and certainly *Bolero* by Ravel has an hypnotic quality. There are moments in much really great music written since the advent of the bar-line when a trance-like state is induced by repetition of rhythmic patterns. Usually, though, this is only ap art of the total effect upon our persons. Not so with jazz, which has been seen as the supreme displacer of inhibitions and intellectual complications. The end product, for many, is the discharge of strong emotion, assisted by violent or prolonged dancing.

> It was with wild hysterical dances that Britain greeted the Armistice in 1918. Negro jazz came as a godsend to the war-neurotics of the period – the waltz and the two-step were not invented for the release of strong emotions.[14]

There is, however, an additional rhythmic element in jazz apart from the pounding of the pulse and the superimposition of different patterns. The device of syncopation appears in any form of jazz as an almost inevitable reaction to the beat. It is worth examining in some detail.

Syncopation

Basically, syncopation is a contradiction of an established accent or beat. The idea of a normal beat stems really from the early seventeenth century and the rise of the regular, metric pulse of the dance movement. In the previous period of fluid vocal lines, without barring or regular accentation apart from that indicated by word rhythms, there was little scope for such a device, since it is impossible to present a contradiction of pulse without first displaying that which is to be defied. It is for this reason that the beat, the basic *formal* element in jazz, is so important. 'Free flight' can only have significance if there is

[14] Sargant, *op. cit.*, p. 62.

such a thing as gravity, and syncopation is freedom from a fixed and limiting force which must either be displayed, or at least remembered. Ever since the regular pulse of the dance set feet tapping all over Europe, syncopation has flourished. A Hornpipe and Sarabande by Lully will serve as a fair example.

Example 2

From a Scarabande

From a Hornpipe

and later - - - -

In each case Lully is combining rhythmic freedom with harmonic tension in the form of suspensions, and the total effect is one of delay, unwilling resolution. Even in the lively, driving Hornpipe, the top part is moving to its proper harmony note after the other parts, displaying a tension-relaxation effect. This device is the distinctive feature of Bach's Two Part Invention in E Major.

Example 3

A very different effect is gained by Handel in the well-known Hornpipe from the *Water Music*.

Example 4

Here, the second beat of the bar is *anticipated* not delayed. As such it is never sounded. The listener and performer automatically respond to the absence of the second beat by supplying it, either mentally or muscularly. It is this type of syncopation that is the basic device in jazz rhythms and those of jazz-derived popular songs.

If we compare the opening of Bach's Three Part Invention in E Minor with *Black and Blue* by 'Fats' Waller, both being thematically similar, the difference will be felt (Example 5). For Bach, the most important beat in the top part is the third, i.e. the *weak* beat. As far as the top part is concerned the stronger first beat of bar 2 does not exist. There is instead a late and almost unwilling resolution of harmonic tension. Waller, on the other hand treats his fourth quaver of the right hand as an *accented note* and leaves it at that, the accompaniment ploughing on in boogie style, providing the strict pulse and incidentally, a duplication of the tune in strict time. In performance, the third quaver is lightened and shortened to help this false accentuation to make effect. It is as though Waller has heaved us some way into the air on his rising phrase, and is leaving us to make our own way down, landing as best we can. If this tune were played by, say, trombones, the 'fall' would be used, a fading *glissando* down from the 'C', ending in indeterminate pitch. Waller controls only the outgoing movement leaving the return to be felt in the muscles of the dancers or listeners, just as Handel does in Example 4. Bach, on the other hand, controls both outward and return movement and whereas in jazz the tone fades after the effect of the syncopation, in classical music of this sort a *crescendo* is implied. Not only this but Bach invites us to contemplate the thematic inversion in the left hand, as though we were spectators viewing two, and later three, sets of carefully controlled movement. An understanding of these fundamental differences will help towards an understanding of the total jazz effect and the basic difference between the jazz and classical ethos. Essentially, the

Example 5

Invention in E Minor

Black and Blue

syncopation of most classical music is a form of terracing, descending in logical steps after the upwards climb of a phrase, while jazz syncopation is more often a bit of extra impetus that pushes us over the top leaving our feelings to roll or tumble down as we will.

It is in the use of this device by solo players that much really exciting jazz is created, since a good musician will improvise an acrobatic descent for us. Those who prefer to dance or fill up the spaces by clicking fingers or tapping feet will resent the intrusion of such a demonstration, because it does not allow such personal, physical response. In fact, the more able and complex the musician becomes, the less popular will be his music and the greater will it resemble, both in technique and feeling, the classical tradition, in the control of the motion to and from the beat. In this way syncopation is representative of the whole jazz situation, in that as soon as jazz goes beyond a certain point from simplicity to complexity it ceases to be itself.

It is worth noting that many percussion instruments, particularly those from Latin America, tend to syncopate without encouragement. The tambourine, the chocolo and the maracas, for example, will rattle as they are drawn back in preparation for the beat, thus providing anticipation unasked for on paper and practically impossible to notate accurately. It is probable that in a similar way the negro origins of jazz provided situations where syncopation in a natural form existed. The preliminary grunt that precedes hard effort, the effort made by sweating slaves, is a form of syncopation that may well have become part of vocal technique in time (especially in work-songs) and later, part of the instrumental expertise of the jazz musician.

The Soul of Jazz

How then does the sum total of beat, sound, improvisation and syncopated rhythm add up to a musical experience? What area of human feeling does jazz explore and reveal? Those who play jazz, and especially those who would place the blues at the heart of jazz, have given an answer. If our need is for music that takes into account the more complex interrelations of form and feeling, then music in the classical tradition will make audible for us these states of being. But if a man's need is

> movement unhampered, unlimited, a free intuitional flow, a spiritual flight as unconcerned with galaxies as it is with the counting of coins, he builds no architecture. On the ground, under the open sky, he sings and dances. He spins endless, inspired, improvised variations in rhythmic sound, yields joyously to that creative stream which is the only ultimate definitive symbol and solvent of time, space and matter. They are the externalization—these moving variations—of pure flight.
>
> He is the Negro come from Africa to America, and this form which directs movement in space, spins out sequential time and gives tone to a soaring pattern, . . . is the humble and profound music we call the blues.[15]

This description comes very close to the attempt, at the start of this book, to describe the real nature of music. Others have spoken of the drum pushing away the world of practical time, and of the continuous, ceaseless creation of a stream of sound. Jazz is best experienced in the 'session', a whole evening or night when the music seems almost to take over our feelings and liberate from confusion and the habitual responses to life situations. The heavy beat is the inflexible ultimate over which is created a dance in sound. It is the interaction between the beat, the simplest of artificial *forms*, with improvised, inflected sound, the freest mode of *expression*, that grips the imagination of the player and the enthusiast. It offers a musical experience to many who have been denied in other ways, either through their own limitations of understanding or because of the retreat of classical composers into formal and experimental ivory towers. It is no criticism to say that jazz is limited. All real music must be limited. Technical restrictions, key structures, thematic economy and all the rest are the very means of building a language, to enable communication to take place. If anything can happen without restriction then no com-

[15] Rudi Blesh, *Shining Trumpets*, pp. 99–101.

munication can take place. It is the creation of a work within a framework of style, vocabulary and grammar that gives it shape and meaning. In jazz, as in anything else, we have to assess the effectiveness of what is happening within the chosen limits. Jazz rarely structures its material above the minimum of the pulse, but at least it has communicated with the mass of people in its time, and for many it is able to satisfy and enthral. The fact that this music does not attempt to present us with a sense of past or future, but confines itself to the immediate present, should not cause us to reject it as a kind of poor relation to the more ordered and larger musical concepts. We must learn to recognise folk-music in whatever form it appears.

Signal or Symbol

We must distinguish between two sorts of jazz lover, or at any rate between two different ways of approaching jazz. When jazz is used for dancing it is often possible to observe these two responses. We can be practically hypnotised by the throbbing beat, which can be heard and felt through the shouting and the shuffling. The improvised solos, if there are any, are often lost in the general din. The trance induced by the pulse can become almost hysterical and terminate in collapse. Credit for this is usually given to alcohol but in many cases the symptoms are helped to a large extent by the music and the dancing. The dancer is indeed 'in flight', 'off the ground', but on real and powerful feelings which are sometimes out of control. The players and group of musical admirers, on the other hand, may well be enjoying the interaction of beat with melodic and rhythmic invention. This is quite different. The shallow listener is using the beat to work upon his actual physical condition, the music being a channel *for* his emotions: the more discerning listener (the one who is really listening) is understanding the improvisation and solo-work as a pattern *of* feelings.

The first mode of response we might well call reaction to a *signal*. The music is a trigger action to start off a chain response in an automatic way, to let off steam, to release emotional tension and to have the company and support of other people with similar needs. Such a use of music cannot really be considered to have much to do with 'Art' in any form. It is a reflection of the immediate mood and though it may bring about a sort of release for a time yet we learn nothing from it. When we wake next morning, apart from a headache it may never have happened. The music here is a mirror, we see our own reflection and nothing beyond.

The second form of response is not just a simple reaction to sound stimuli. Feelings may be reflected in part but we are able to see through the glass in places and become aware of the motion of our feelings. The music can reveal to us something of our own nature and this is often deeply satisfying, for it gives us a sense of identity and at the same time an understanding of outside forces pressing upon our own selves. Something of this, though the description be impossible, is present in any truly musical experience and its effects linger beyond the hangover stage. Jazz knows its limits. Its rhythms prepare only for the immediate future, the world is narrowed to the next beat, what is to come is only half a breath from what is now. We are shown a hectic, pulsating present. There is value here of an aesthetic kind. We could say that it is an elemental or 'primary' sort of music; it certainly can be understood by simple and primitive peoples. Yet though its range is small, if successfully presented it can be a source of enlightenment as well as relief.

We all undergo on a small scale daily, and in larger ways over longer periods of time, forms of regression, when it seems that a state of crisis is reached before new ideas and adjustments are possible. We say 'I'm not on form today', or 'I need time to sort myself out'. This is the purpose of the blues, the office of the best of jazz, and it cannot be ignored. Personality needs such moments of simplification and in this way the rise of jazz complements the work of Freud. To use jazz as *music* is to experience a *symbolic* presentation of our own inner and dynamic life, stripped of its civilised and intellectual complexities. Jazz musicians who feel strongly this element of their work will often resent the use of jazz in inferior ways or as a grass root of popular music.

Jazz and Pop

The very mention of popular or 'commercial' music in front of a jazz musician provokes, quite often, a verbal storm. Indeed, the jazz lover is much more sensitive in this direction than the classical musician because the public are liable to react to jazz in the inadequate way described above, and because so many of the recurrent clichés in popular and dance music stem from the basic jazz vocabulary. Blesh writes of commercial music:

> Everywhere its strangling pressure is felt, in the limited symphonic repertory and the gagging of the new composer, who can scarcely achieve public hearing; in the increasing banality of popular music, and in the appearance of swing, an aural activity devoted to neurotic excitement and the cliché. Such classical music as survives in the commercial repertory fares well enough, in a sterile sort of way, protected by its unalterable score and its traditional interpretation. But true jazz, which must be improvised by inspired and devoted players, withers in such an atmosphere.[16]

According to Blesh, Whiteman, Gershwin and Paul Robeson have corrupted the jazz scene. This is an extreme position and possibly the most honest and discerning and modified versions of it exist among many writers and players. Brubeck[17] would like us to hear more good music from all true sources, including classical music, the theatre, folk music and jazz 'instead of being force-fed on juke-box versions'.

In spite of the strained relations between jazz and pop it is a fact that they so manage to survive through a queer kind of

[16] *Shining Trumpets*, pp. 11–12.
[17] Article in *Punch*, May 1964.

dependence on each other. Popular music needs jazz to provide it with a certain historical status and many basic idiomatic ideas, and the jazz musician needs money. There are not many jazz players today able to live on fees paid for 'inspired, improvised variations', though many play the 'real thing' for their own pleasure whilst extracting from the public, by way of dance-hall and pop recording, the necessary bread and butter. Only a few manage to remain passionately anti-commercial: the rest grumble but submit.

Not only is the pure jazz player something of a rarity but so also are his listeners. There may be a lot of people within earshot, but even if this is so the vast proportion of them will be attending to the music in the poorer of the two ways mentioned above. Because of the small public the player often has to accept engagements or 'gigs' at dances or at best in clubs where he will be expected to play 'standards', the well-known pieces. This limitation is often imposed by those who enjoy jazz but it is very constricting, since it implies the ability and possibility of repeat performances. This is just not possible for anyone who claims to create his music on the spot, spontaneously. Small wonder that many are pessimistic about the chances of jazz surviving this century.

The jazz page of *Melody Maker*[18] asked for opinions on the present situation, as far as work is concerned, from those involved with 'plain honest dance music', not even thoroughgoing jazz. Even for the older sort of dance band, largely composed of jazz enthusiasts, things are very difficult at times due to the employment of pop groups instead of the more traditional ensemble. The general opinion at that time seemed to be that 'the public have been brainwashed into accepting the ridiculous by the musical industry'. A well-known jazz player in the same magazine[19] later on said that jazz would die and he was beginning to listen more and more to classical music on

[18] November 1963.
[19] Bruce Turner, February 1964.

records. Several other articles at various times reported empty chairs in places where jazz is played. Fairly recently the following figures were given, based on record sales in America:[20]

Popular music	49·1 per cent
Classical music	18·9 per cent
Hot jazz	0·8 per cent

Whatever the future holds for jazz there is no doubt that it has influenced popular music during this century and to some extent classical music too. It has greatly increased the range of expression and technique and has instigated a new rhythmic feeling. The device of syncopation and the mood of the blues has been absorbed by musical comedy writers. Furthermore, it displays a wide range of possibilities from the dance-hall to the intellectual and esoteric modern groups. No teacher of music can ignore its implications, for jazz has not only played the main role of the 'low' music in our century but is also striving to integrate with the 'high'. Its chief virtue though is that it has provided earthy sounds, full of expressive quality, in an age that may well be too elaborate in its artistic pretensions.

[20] Given by F. Newton, *The Jazz Scene*.

CHAPTER 3

POPULAR SONG—THE MUSIC

Concerning the Beatles:
"They have brought a distinctive and exhilarating flavour into a
genre of music that was in danger of ceasing to be music at all."[1]
The Times

ONE great difficulty in trying to describe the musical nature of
most pop products is that, like jazz, the experience of such
music is only to be found during the moments of performance
and is elusive in print. In format and general appearance a
present-day pop song resembles many other pieces published
over the last thirty years or more, yet in performance there are
often striking differences. The reason for this continuity of
notation tradition is not so hard to find. When, earlier on, jazz
musicians set down music on paper, or more likely, when what
they played was arranged for the public use by other people,
the conventional notation that was familiar in Sousa marches
and imported popular tunes was brought into use. On paper a
Sullivan song and a slow blues may well share many common
attributes – the left hand of the piano part hopping about with
an 'um-cha, um-cha' effect, for example – but in performance
it becomes clear that the pieces represent respectively two
entirely different worlds of culture and tradition. The devious
ways of altering rhythm and sound were passed on aurally,
through performance, and later the recording. The essence of
jazz, or those popular numbers rooted in jazz, is not in what is
written but in what is played, and as a result the copies often
look thin and unconvincing. The same might be said of printed
versions of the older type of folk-song. To name just one common

[1] Music critic of *The Times*, December 27th, 1963.

discrepancy, it is certain that most jazz pieces are, in performance, in compound time although they are invariably printed
in simple time. *Doctor Jazz* (Example 1) written in 4/4 would be
played in 12/8 time. A related factor here is, that as far as
publishers are concerned, no copy should be too difficult for
the purchasing public to unravel. This attitude tends to
standardise accompaniment figurations and the range and
speed of decoration, which boils down to a stylised and petrified
'improvisation'.

For these reasons neither jazz nor jazz-derived pop arouses
the kind of excitement on paper that the score of Beethoven's
First Symphony is said to have caused in Elgar and the
Ninth in Wagner. When young people buy sheet-music, it
is only as a rough guide to assist a readier imitation of the
particular artist whose picture will be displayed on the
front cover. Pop these days is essentially an aural transmission.
Where in 'Woolworths' once stood the music counter is now
the Record Bar. Remembering the limitations of the notation
and assuming familiarity with the 'sound' of the music in
question it is just possible to describe the elements of certain
popular styles. The Beatles have been chosen frequently as
examples for several reasons. They have, so far, been in the
public eye for six years, they caused in 1964 the situation known
as 'Beatlemania', and they display a wider range of style and a
much better quality than so many other groups of performers.
How did it all begin?

We have already, in an earlier chapter, briefly traced the
popular tradition as far as the first half of the twentieth century. Since 1948 there have been on the popular music market
many revivals of musical comedy tunes of the older kind and
some new productions, with emphasis on the open-air, healthy,
American way of life (*Oklahoma*; *Annie Get Your Gun*). Sometimes, usually pathetically, a tragic note is sounded in these
musicals (*Carousel*). The 'stars' of these shows and of the growing film industry were the idols of the 1940's, and boyish girls,

Doris Day for example, were popular. Later, the 'crooner' became fashionable as a kind of inward-turning after a period of extrovertion. Donald Peers was followed in the 1950's by Johnny Ray singing *Cry*. After another spell of more lively preferences (*Guys and Dolls*; *Kiss Me Kate*; *The King and I*) in 1956, that crucial year, 'Rock 'n Roll' appeared. The whole trend was begun by the film *Rock Around The Clock*, an American production, and it is probably the last of the great fashions in popular culture to be launched in the cinema. Since then films have assisted the spread of popularity of specific idols, but the spearhead of the attack has been the gramophone record, the wireless and television programme, the public performance and the literature about all three. Largely because of growing teenage affluence, along with the rest of the Western society, the sales of records grew rapidly and many groups were formed with expensive equipment to reproduce the sound and the beat of 'Rock'. In spite of a short-lived attempt to be 'folksy' with 'skiffle' and tea-chest basses, the trend from the middle 1950's has been towards group playing and singing of songs derived from jazz, but amplified through electronic apparatus. From a lively amateur scene in Liverpool emerged the Beatles, heros of 1963 and after.

The Times published its famous article of praise and analysis, and the *Musical Times*[2] rejoiced that at last here were pop singers of a different quality from the rest, 'closer to the instinctual art of the country blues, relatively uncorrupted by Hollywooden cliché'. Even the jazz world found nice things to say:

> For the first time in my life I find myself enjoying the current pop trend. The sentimental sincerity of Vera Lynn; the jolly hiccups of Alma Cogan; the slaughter of the English language by Adam Faith; the shared agony of Billy Fury—all aroused nothing more than a slight sinking feeling in the stomach.
>
> The Beatles have given pop music a gaiety and zest that vanished with the old music halls.[3]

---

[2] July 1964. An article by Wilfred Mellers.
[3] Bob Dawbarn, Jazz critic of *Melody Maker*, November 23rd, 1963.

These views, from different parts of the world of music, serve to show the enthusiasm that is generated when popular music turns, as it does from time to time, back to its roots in entertainment, in gaiety, or in jazz. It would be as well to look first at the music that had 'almost ceased to be music' before the Beatles arrived. Through the line of operetta the lighter pieces of Sullivan, the songs of Bishop, musical comedy, the film and the record industry had emerged a popular music, *classically* derived, which had little in common with the 'instinctual art of the country blues'. It is better to take a specific example rather than to generalise and we may as well begin with Alma Cogan.

Classical Derivations

With You In Mind was published in 1961 and, like similar numbers, coexisted with the more jazzy songs (Example 6).

Example 6

The first four bars (Example 6) would not look bad if laid out for string quartet, so classical is the appearance. There is no trace of either a heavy beat or syncopation. The low, held major seventh at the end of the first bar reminds one briefly of Elgar, and the rocking accompaniment figure in the left-hand of the piano transcription is present throughout the song as a kind of motif. The closing section contains a relatively pure use of the flat sixth in the bass, some restraint being used to avoid the more common 'neapolitan' sixth and to substitute a less eruptive, cleaner alternative (Example 7).

Example 7

The whole song begs for a string orchestra and a round, smooth singing tone. The second bar of Example 6 contains a typical horn progression up the harmonic series, and the phrasing is in regular four-bar periods throughout. Whereas a 'straight' musician might make a poor job of transmitting the sense of a 'beat' number, he could make this song sound reasonable, since the style is close to the tradition he understands. In performance this type of song is often stretched in tempo, *rubato* being the rule, in contrast to the (ideally) immovable jazz-beat. Sometimes such a taking of liberties goes on, that the end product is very much a vehicle for the emotional message of the singer, sometimes little more than a controlled sob. Crosby, Ray, Danny Williams, Peers, and more recently, Presley, have all employed such material in this kind of way. It has a background, well described by Hoggart,[4] of working-class entertainers performing in clubs and pubs. It is a fact that a pianist in a club is able to take any song, old or new, and translate it 'into the received idiom'. Gracie Fields was an expert in this manner (Example 8).

[4] R. Hoggart, *The Uses of Literacy*.

Example 8

Sal - ly   Sal - ly,   Pride of   our   al - - ley -

Something of this extreme flexibility is present in nearly all popular songs that are not rhythmically stabilised around a beat. There is a difference here between the way in which the notation relates to the performance compared with this relationship as manifested in jazz-based songs. In Example 6 the song begins with the composer's notation, as does a classical piece, and is 'interpreted' by the performer, while in the case of a beat group number the notation is, like that of jazz, only an approximate guide, or record of what is put together sound by sound.

Classical, or to be more accurate, 'Romantic' music of the last century abounds with examples of tunes that lend themselves to this expressive treatment, and sometimes they get it too. Look at this tune from Tchaikovsky[5] (Example 9).

Example 9

Tchaikovsky apparently did not feel able to trust unbending classical players to interpret the feeling of the music and so he went to great trouble to indicate just what sort of stretching should be applied to his tune. 'A steady speed, in a singing

[5] From the second movement of the Fifth Symphony.

manner, with some freedom', would seem to indicate a certain liberty of expression, but he goes on to indicate what and where liberties are to be taken. In particular we may notice the un-usual feature of the *tenuto* (held) marking under the last quaver in many of the bars. This, the twelfth quaver, would normally be the least important, lightly played, the music in motion towards the next strong beat. Not so here. It is difficult to explain the effect of this bulge in the wrong part of the bar and phrase. If, in crude analogy, we imagine a verbal cliché to the first five notes of the tune we might well have this: 'Darling I love you.' It makes the flesh creep but it serves. If we float gently through the pronoun towards the verb, we will have shaped the phrase as a whole with the minimum of sentimental effect. If, on the other hand, we obey the composer's instruc-tions, the word 'I' becomes important and some of the linger-ing, caressing emotive charge generated by the *tenuto* is passed on to the strong beat. The impression is of self-expression; the important factor being *not* the object of desire but the feelings of the desiring singer, the lover. Even when we take away the words and treat the phrase as pure music, the effect of hanging about, lingering before the expected accent, is that of savouring one musical second at the expense of the overall shape. Again, the *animando* in the fifth bar and the pull-back later on reminds one of Hoggart's description of the 'big-dipper' style of singing in clubs and theatres where 'the voice takes enormous lifts and dips to fill out the lines of a lush emotional journey'. Whereas many classical players today tend to iron out these bulges, the popular singer who has learned his musical manners from the tradition of the 'big-dipper' thrives on squeezing the last drop of 'expression' out of the tunes he sings or plays.

Not all popular music stems from jazz, and those pieces that do not owe a great deal to the plushier classical composers. Two illustrations of opposite attitudes come to mind.

> The more enthusiastic his audience is, why the more spirit the work-ing man's got to play. And with your natural feelings that way you

never make the same thing twice. Every time you play a new tune ideas come to mind and you slip that one in.

[Johnny St. Cyr—the jazz banjo player.]

Compare this statement with the following:

My whole trick is to keep the tune well out in front. If I play Tchaikovsky I play his melodies and skip his spiritual struggles. Naturally I condense. I have to know just how many notes my audience will stand for. If there's time left over I fill in with a lot of runs up and down the keyboard.   [Liberace.][6]

Clearly the first example is of a sincere, expressive approach, while the second is of a commercial attitude, a dilution to the greatest common denominator of well-tried formal music, the excrescence of the 'high' music of the last century. To bend tunes that best serve a formal purpose as part of a larger structure, or to write tunes that evoke the superficial elements of the classical tradition and then stretch them like rock, is to achieve neither a real reflection of our times nor a genuine artistic experience. It is far better, surely, to create expressive sounds, bounded only (for the best players) by a pulse and catching the more immediate feelings of the audience: in other words, a small genuine article without pretensions is likely to be more truly valuable than any imitation of a tiny part of the work of a bygone age. It is to the credit of our adolescents that they have supported trends recently away from this corruption to something which at least has the possibility of being alive. It is to this that we now turn.

Jazz-derived Pop

We have seen something of the possible power of jazz to cause excitement and we have noted opinions of those who find it stimulating. It is useful to look at the 'beaty' sort of popular song to see just how much of it is true to the technique and spirit of jazz. A comparison between the classic *Doctor Jazz* (Example 1) and a fairly typical selection of pop tunes in the

[6] Quoted in *The Popular Arts*, S. Hall and P. Whannel.

1960's will help. In the former we notice the dotted rhythms common to jazz and military marches. In performance the speed gives a steady, swinging motion. The bass part has a life of its own, moving in contrary motion to the tune and laying down as it goes the foundation for the rich, hymn-tune harmony.

These harmonies were conceived under the hands of a pianist, the instrumental technique determining to a large degree the mode of the musical expression. We may notice the little figuration at the phrase-end in the third bar, a hint of improvisation that would blossom on the clarinet or trumpet in performance. The blues feeling is strong especially in the second bar when the lowered third note of the scale, typical of the blues, is harmonised by a 'German Sixth', a chord well suited to this sort of feeling. All through the piece the left hand drives on whilst over the top the music 'swings' along.

A similar sort of effect can be found in *Ev'rybody's Twistin'* which is sung by Sinatra[7] (Example 10). The tune is as old as 1935, when it appeared as *Truckin'*.

Example 10

Listen you fellow twist- - - - ers   Listen and hear me through- -

[7] 1962.

A typical guitar suggestion appears in the introductory bar; the left hand fingers form a pattern while the right hand makes a regular up and down movement. All musicians worth their salt exploit to some degree the instrument they are using. Notice the flattened seventh, a device with the same dragging quality as the lowered third, and the built-in syncopation. There is quite an amount of jazz feeling here, in spite of the words. Compare now these two pieces with something much closer to the heart of the pop world[8] (Example 11).

Example 11

I'm in pieces,   bits and pieces   Since you left me and you   said good - bye - - -   etc.

Here are the outward signs of jazz, the dotted rhythms and four-in-a-bar, but the whole melodic and harmonic design is much simpler, the speed is faster and there is much less feeling of improvisation. In close analysis we find that only *two* chords are used in the first thirty-two bars compared with *eight* chords in the first *two* bars of *Doctor Jazz*. The bass part is an *ostinato*, an incantation which proclaims 'A-men' thirty-two times, and over the top is a tune that for all but eight bars uses only *four* notes. There is no syncopation anywhere. Clearly, this song belongs to the dance hall and exists primarily to provoke a response of a physical nature among the audience. The result may be beneficial, but it could hardly be called interesting from a purely musical point of view. Yet songs like this have tremendous power in performance upon those who worship the singers, and have learned the communal response.

[8] *Bits and Pieces*, The Dave Clark Five, 1961.

It is in the light of songs that have minimal musical content that the Beatles appear so significant, and the writer makes no apology for using this group as examples more than any other. There happens to be more to say about them. They use the worn harmony of the last century as we have found it in jazz, but they often go a little further with some striking progressions, that, in context, sound quite fresh. *Hold Me Tight*, for example (Example 12, by permission of Northern Songs Ltd., 1963).

Example 12

Not only is the blues minor third in a major key used here but it is harmonised as the root of an ordinary triad.

This use of harmony is not a result of the study of classical or jazz models but, once more, largely stems from guitar technique, where there are no 'black notes' but only chord patterns which easily become chromatic by sliding the hand up and down. These progressions have been used at times in sensitive ways and with some artistry by the Beatles. The 'autocratic but by no means ungrammatical attitude to tonality', lauded by *The Times*, is largely a product of technical possibilities combined with a good ear, which is what expressive music is all about. Here again is the stamp of the folk-singer.

Other typical Beatle traits include a pretty throroughgoing use of syncopation (Example 13, *Can't Buy Me Love*, 1964.

Example 13

Can't Buy Me Love (1964)

Buy you a diamond ring— my friend if it makes you feel all right   etc.

Sometimes the group falls back on the cruder device of mere pace and drive to provoke physical response, and a sort of chorus opportunity for the audience. *Money*, is an example. It is not one of the group's home-made numbers and the copy tells one very little about the performance, when the incantation reaches hypnotic proportions. The high-priest shouts 'Money!' and the worshippers reply with, 'That's what I want'. Their better songs are in fact written by Lennon and Mc-Cartney and display quite remarkable invention and freshness. They achieve something of a feeling of 'free flight' in the melismatic effects which they have made their own. By altering and extending the verbal syllables they carry on to some extent the tradition of the older blues singers when they experimented with timbre and pitch (Examples 14, 15, 16).

Example 14

All I've Got To Do (1963)

When ev- er I - - - - - - - - - - - - - - etc.

All I gotta do - - - - - - - - - - - - - - - etc.

Example 15

She Loves You (1963)

Yes - ter- - day-yi - yay

Example 16

Hold Me Tight (1963)

You   you   you - oo - oo - oo   oo.

We might notice other qualities of this particular group before moving on to look at the more general aspects of popular music. Anyone familiar with the Beatles will have been impressed by the wide vocal range, the strange and sometimes striking words and the variety of approach. Above all they display an unusual control over speed and feeling which prevents their numbers from becoming either sentimental or just nonsensical. There are many elements here of recognisable folk-song practice.

The Customer

It might be said that adolescents who fall at the feet of pop groups are not concerned with such refinements, and indeed, for many of them such details pass almost unnoticed. Remember though that hundreds of amateur groups have practised for long hours to try to make the kind of music described above. Whatever the motives for beginning, some sort of *musical* satisfaction must have entered into the sessions at some stage or other. We are reminded of the cave-men drawing for magical reasons on the stone walls: ultimately, interest and enjoyment of the activity *for itself* seems to have taken over from the cruder drives of fear and hunger.

The writer has noticed among our school-children a promising reaction. When a pop song was being played on the gramophone, at times and for a brief moment a whole section of the class would suddenly, at a certain moment, quietly sing or hum with the music. Just for a second or two, before relapsing back into the semi-bored attitude seen on pop television programmes, the music had lifted the pupils out of themselves. In nearly every instance it would be possible to point to an attractive turn of melody, or a melismatic or instrumental effect which was felt to be musically effective. Many young people of 14 and over have expressed the view that they 'wait for bits to come'. For example, 'I like it when he sings "merci" and when he rolls his tongue'. One boy made a comparison between popular songs that he liked and Armstrong's *Potato Head Blues*, saying that with the latter he listened 'all through' but in the pop songs he only really listened to certain parts. This degree of appreciation is quite removed from the waves of screaming that, without musical cause, sweep through crowds of adolescent girls at concerts. Sometimes a physical gesture by the performer sets it going, but at other times it is simply a chain-reaction among the audience without specific reference to either performers or music as such.

Just as in the places where jazz is played some will dance and some will crowd the band hoping for a musical revelation, so in pop we must distinguish between two types of listener, often both in the same person, one chasing a form of excitement devoid of art, the other on his way to becoming a discriminating patron. Eventually the latter will move away in search of richer things. Keeping him in mind, it will be useful to pinpoint some of the general weaknesses that popular music embraces in order to make itself acceptable as 'mass culture'. A brief look at some of the processes involved in its production will indicate the direction in which we should turn to find the reasons behind the more violent and disturbing symptoms that bother parents and teachers.

In the first place there is a chain of producers and retailers behind most pop songs that is long and complex out of all proportion to the music as such. It is no longer a question of the musician standing and improvising for his audience until he has no more to say. Between the musical idea and the public at present there is a complex filter, by-passed by only a few. To begin with, the singer and composer are usually two separate entities. The composing, initially, is often a matter of picking out a tune on the piano and then turning it over to a syndicate for harmonisation and arrangement. At this stage quite a lot of professional expertise goes into shaping up the song to conform to a standard which seems to be commercially viable. The singers, who will have begun as amateurs, have to find a manager who in turn may run a 'stable' where grooming, rehearsal and selection take place. The next stage is to find a man with influence on recording companies; he is usually called the Artists and Repertory man (A and R man), and he will often suggest changes in the material or refuse to handle a particular performer on the grounds that he will not 'go over'. Once this hurdle is over and the singer and song are united with recording company, further modifications take place in the hands of the engineers, who can pick out certain elements of the sound and reinforce them, or splice the tape, mixing together various bits from different performances to produce what they feel is an overall acceptable disc. Leaving alone for the moment the advertising and outlets for the product, it is clear that any song that is put through this process, and many are, must lose some of its vitality, if it had any, to become acceptable to the largest number and offensive to no one. This is one of the less happy features of democracy. There is a tendency for the material to be pruned into the mediocre third rate, tolerated by most people but able, under its own steam, to thrill no one.

A few points will serve to indicate the musical results of such a system and attitude. The standard by which we judge, jazz-derived pop is its ability to get 'off the ground' and into flight. Jazz is concerned with the immediate, energetic response to the passing of time, the passing of Fate, the movement of the beat. Empathy with the performer as he sweats and strains to break out over this pulse, into wild and colourful activity in terms of rhythm and sound is, for many, an essential condition for a real and vital jazz experience. How does popular music match up to this intensity?

Instead of stretching rhythmic potential, with the resultant effects of muscular exhilaration and sense of bodily freedom, battery-produced pop music is designed not to confuse those who listen with half an ear. Consequently, sustained flights of improvisation, or even the motions of syncopation are avoided. Rhythms are usually simple, and when any more elaborate melody appears it is usually in the form of mere embellishment, and not a kind of melodic adventure. Even the drive in the rhythm is not of the same order as the swing of jazz. The beat is not produced by the straining arms, or exerted vocal or instrumental sources, it is more a matter of recorded volume.

In a similar way, the personality of the pop singer need not come into play; instead, he simply projects the image built for him and round him by the 'ad. man'. Neither the noise nor the personal effect is effected by the stress and strain of a communicating performer. If this were so we could identify ourselves with his struggle for expression, we could achieve empathy, our muscles tightening and our blood coursing with his as he defies human limitations of prosaic gravity and finds and shows us the poetry of flight through his exertions. One virtue at least belongs to the dancing witch-doctor, leading his tribe to hysteria and catharsis; he pours out energy sufficient to lead the dance that will both exhaust and satisfy the believers. In this case it is not often so. The triumph belongs to the electronics industry and the recording companies. It is they who create and sustain the sound and amplify the beat; it is they who are able to project the 'open skies' sensation by the use of echo chambers, and to present 'continuous creation' in terms of the 'fade-out'. So important are the technical aids to some performers that they are often unable to risk live performance at all. Records are the result of many tape splicings and on television, 'stars' mime the words to their own recording while the studio audience contrive, not always with much success, to look 'sent'.

These sorts of limitations are not always present and in the very best pop music they do not apply. Some records become popular for genuine musical merits, Brubeck's *Take Five* for example, and have never been processed in the ways described. But apart from the odd really effective piece and the small but discriminating audiences, the *music* of so many popular successes has little or no power in *purely* musical terms, to assume the proportions of a 'problem' for parents or teachers. There are some clues worth noting in the words of these songs that will lead to a clearer understanding of the position.

The Words

Basically, we can divide up the lyrics into three broad categories. The obvious one is that concerned with 'love' in one way or another. We should expect and welcome this, since it is obvious that adolescents have to come to grips sooner or later with the problem of relationships with the other sex. Just as a younger child may draw or play at being an animal of which he is afraid, so here is a chance for the young adult to familiarise himself with the various aspects of a very important part of his ever-expanding experience. Consequently we have songs ranging from the coy and sentimental to the downright erotic and inflammatory.

'Don't do that, please stop it, please stop it now.'

'Stay awhile, till I've told you Ooh!
Of the love that I feel tonight.'

Sometimes the sentiments and even the text of older songs are revived to illuminate the basic theme. An interesting example is the use of the German folk-tune *Muss i denn*, with its rather mushy words, by Presley, under the title *Wooden Heart*. There is not really much to chose between:

Muss i denn, muss i denn zumm Stadtele 'naus,
Und du, mein Schatz bleibst hier?[9]

And the following:

And if you say goodbye, then I know that I would cry.

Or between either and the school music book version of the original:

I must journey away through the dark winter's day,
With the snow and tears half blind.[10]

We either sympathise or we do not.

This sort of song really belongs to the second category, that of songs of lost love, which is really the other side of the same coin. In general such songs are not quite so healthy as those that emphasise the positive aspects of human relationships. Sentimentality enters in to a greater degree. It is, however, the third group of songs that claims our attention, since it is not quite so easy to find anything quite like it in previous musical history. We could discover plenty of Schubert songs of love and lost love but hardly one with these sort of implications.

'Listen you fellow twisters,
Listen and hear me through.'

Everyone is invited into the fellowship of the dance, we can all 'belong' if we 'twist'. Lyrics of this kind are plentiful and can

[9] Must I then leave the town, and you, my darling, remain here?
[10] *Oxford School Music Book*. Senior Preliminary.

be found in jazz. Constant Lambert[11] complained about this sort of song with 'its hysterical emphasis on the fact that the singer is a jazz baby going crazy about jazz rhythms'. A large number of pop songs have the same basic message of 'togetherness', for example, *Twist and Shout* and *Rock Around the Clock*. This is important, for they display a self- and group-consciousness typical of the adolescent.

> This inward-turning, self-pitying quality of many of the slower teenage ballads, the community-of-lost-souls feeling invoked in words and rhythms, is both an authentic rendering of the adolescent mood and a stylized exaggeration of it.[12]

It is in fact a part of the teenager's struggle to find and hold symbols of belonging in the world and in the community. Love and lost love-songs explore for him the new world of sex and romance; identification with such pieces is very strong. The 'with it' type of number stimulates feelings of group solidarity, which provides some anchorage in the deep and troublesome waters of personal change from child to adult. Words with a simple chorus-like response; tunes that are all out of the same mould; rhythms that promote a simple, universal reaction: all these factors are part of the satisfaction of a need for security.

As for the music itself, we have seen that the beat, the sound and the hints of exploration in improvisation and melisma *can* have artistic significance. Some teenagers, especially older people, undoubtedly appreciate some of the best pop in the same way that they are beginning to understand Beethoven. Often the songs have little if anything to say, but sometimes they do and if so we should be glad. However, for the most part the musical element of such pieces is not strong enough to cause either pleasure or rioting, and we must look a little further for those attributes that send teenagers into hysteria, and seriously affect the work of any parent or teacher who would like to show them other music and new experiences. It is the

[11] *Music Ho!*
[12] *The Popular Arts.*

use to which popular music is put, rather than its artistic content that will explain how it acts upon those who find it potent. For a few, at certain times, pop music may well offer a *symbol-structure* of the more immediate and ephemeral feelings, and sometimes it may take us even further if we care to really listen. But for the many who purchase and play, it is a *sign-language*, signifying which role is to be played by the group of admirers to best maintain unity and security. In this case it is a rather simple linking mechanism, and it rarely is able to break its chains and explore the larger world outside.

CHAPTER 4

POPULAR SONG—THE CULTURE

"... music has for centuries been an effective agent for intro-
ducing "group solidarity"—whether the occasion be the Peace
of Aix-la-Chappelle, the opening of the Manchester Ship Canal,
or the Cup Final at Wembley."[1]   MACKERNESS

ANY account of music and its effect on human feeling that
attempts to demonstrate absolute and predictable physical
reactions to particular sounds is doomed to failure. It is
possible to show that music has, at times and for certain people,
affected pulse-rate, respiration and even metabolism, but such
effects are by no means universal and usually are determined
to a large extent by the learned responses of the individual in
question. The same pieces, for example, would have a different
effect if played to a man from a remote Indian village than
they would if performed for the benefit of a London suburban
music-club. It is important to keep this musical relativity in
mind, when looking at the more violent effects of popular music
on our younger people. To get the full benefit of any piece we
must first know the style, that is to say, we must understand the
vocabulary and grammar of what we hear. Only then can
exciting deviations or extensions of the language be appreciated
and enjoyed. This 'knowing' is not just an intellectual thing
but is largely a question of feeling the significance of the piece
in its context, and of feeling the import of each part of the piece
in relation to the whole. This way of knowing music is the
ultimate in enjoyment and understanding of the composer's
intentions, and we have seen in the previous chapter that the

[1] E. D. Mackerness, *A Social History of English Music.*

great bulk of popular music has little to offer in this direction. Some of it though is well worth attention and we shall come to some specific virtues later on. However, for the moment we must try to clarify the issue as to what it is that popular music stands for in the case of adolescents. If only we could say that this particular chord, or that specific rhythm, generates this or that feeling. But it is not so.

> If there were a one-to-one relationship between the physical sound and the mental experience which it elicits, our problem would be simplified. However, such relationships scarcely if ever exist. The mental response never corresponds exactly to the physical event, . . . the listener may put a great deal more into music than was originally intended or is actually present in the musical form, as, for example, the vivacious responses to primitive tom-toms or to present-day ragtime.[2]

Not only do we take from music that which we have learned by experience to enjoy, but we also read into it personal wishes and likings, and other factors which were probably never present in any way in the mind of the composer. This is not only the case with popular music or 'primitive tom-toms' but also with classical music. Farnsworth[3] relates the story of the Danish broadcasting company, who doubled their listening ratings for one programme simply by changing its title from 'Classical' to 'Popular'. The music continued as before but the audience brought to it different expectations, they were prepared to enjoy it because of its label and so, apparently, they did.

The suggestion that the music would, under its new heading, be liked by more people had done its work. A more striking example is cited by Brown.[4] He tells of an experiment in an American high school, where only 96 per cent of the students recognised the same portion of Brahms's First Symphony played twice as being, in fact, the same piece. They were told by someone they considered to be an expert that the second playing was an inferior imitation. Most students agreed with the

[2] C. E. Seashore, *Psychology of Music*, pp. 378 ff.
[3] P. R. Farnsworth, *The Social Psychology of Music*.
[4] J. A. C. Brown, *Techniques of Persuasion*.

'expert', some suspended judgement and the rest disagreed. Other examples can be recalled, including the sudden unpopularity of music from Germany during the First World War. Some people at this time found that Beethoven was not really such a fine composer as they had previously imagined.

So it is clear that, whatever else it may be, music is a commodity without a clear label to indicate when or how it should be used. This is why people react differently to the same piece, why critics differ enormously at times in their reviews of performances and why popular music can be drowned in the screams of teenagers or taken quietly to heart at home. Even if a work is clearly conceived by the composer and faithfully transmitted by the performer, yet, a faulty receiver – the inadequate listener – can make nonsense of it. We should not be surprised then if music is sometimes deployed in ways that seem less than satisfactory to the purist. We must remember, though, that the misuse of a piece need not indicate a bad composition, but merely a poor set of audience expectations. After all, it would not be hard to find at opera, ballet, or the Festival Hall those whose motives for being there were to do with social habit and status, or the preference of a friend or sweetheart, rather than for any specifically musical reason.

So let us be clear that any sort of music can be heard in different ways, for different reasons and with different effects on the behaviour of the listeners. We not only extract from music what we have learned to like but we also tend to read into it what we expect or need to find. The pop-music world provides outstanding examples. A participant at a concert in a northern town recalls that, when Helen Shapiro was 'at the top', the audience listened to her songs and received them enthusiastically but practically ignored one of the long-haired supporting groups who, a few months later, became nationally known as the Beatles. Yet one would imagine that the songs they sang then were not so very different from those which

later took on the power to disturb and excite audiences in such
an extreme manner. One of the psychological mechanisms at
work here is 'suggestion', and we have already seen it at work
in different ways. To be effective, suggestion of any kind has to
be directed towards existing needs and desires. It is impossible
to suggest any action or reaction to a person who does not
believe that certain wishes or desires will be satisfied by such
behaviour. It is possible, indeed inevitable, that many adults
react violently *against* the implied suggestions of pop music. In
fact, primitive drumming and ritual, and the effects of regular
flashing lights can be resisted by those who do not wish to be
involved or enter a trance-like state.

> People are deeply excited by drumming and chanting, not by the
> mechanical effect alone, but because *they believe in the particular creed that
> they signify* and permit themselves to pass into a state of frenzy. [Writer's
> italics.] That, indeed, is generally their object in attending the
> meeting.[5]

This very neatly sums up the hold and position of popular
music in the life of our adolescents, and we must now have
some idea of the 'creed' to which they would subscribe.

The Needs of Young People

Adults are often forgetful of their own adolescent experience,
and of the discomfort and mental pain that is often present at
this time. Indeed, it may be said that the unpleasantness is of
such an order that 'forgetting' is the natural psychological
reaction. One of the problems at this stage of development is a
certain confusion and doubt as to the place and use of newly
developing feelings and attitudes. The great difficulty is to
find an adult role without adult experience, and to find some
kind of satisfactory position on the community. There is also
the need to contain and understand the strong emotional

[5] Brown, *op. cit.*, p. 305.

drives, that sometimes practically cripple the possibility of normal communication with other people, particularly the closer relatives. Tensions appear, not between simple 'good' and 'bad', but between old and newer forms of behaviour. Naturally enough, whenever some relief can be found it is accepted.

The most potent orientating factor is often known as the 'peer-group' relationship. To the teacher or parent this may mean apparently mysterious behaviour in the company of others of the same age. Other teenagers generally do not make claims or inflict responsibilities, neither do they expect an adult standard of ability or ethics which, although desirable, is often unattainable at this time.[6] Not only does this herding together of adolescents give them something of a sense of security, a feeling of belonging, but it also provides opportunity for leadership and discipleship. Certain individuals, on the strength of superior prowess or some force of personality, are able to represent the aims and motives of the group which they lead.[7] Not only does membership of such a group give security and some opportunity of this sort, but it does also make it unnecessary to worry overmuch about standards and habits of other social groups. In other words, a sub-culture is formed with its own standards and mores.

At the same time there is a growing sense of social interactions, learned, to a large extent, through the group's activities and through certain types of books, films and plays. Usually the stories that are most acceptable contain a somewhat over-simple hero-figure amongst other characters who also tend to be either good or bad without very much shading off. It is a black and white world in the earlier stages. The hero usually suffers a little before eventually triumphing over his enemies. Quite often the suffering takes the form of being misunderstood by other people until the vindicating truth is finally known. Adolescents are, of course, not the only people who use literature and other media

[6] C. B. Zachry, *Emotion and Conduct in Adolescence*.
[7] C. M. Fleming, *Adolescence*, p. 165.

for the purposes of 'wish-fulfilment', identifying themselves with the central figure and living vicariously his triumph and esteem. The readers of 'Westerns' and women's magazines are making the same diversion from reality because they find it hard to bear.

The transposition of this factor into the realm of popular music is quite easy. It seems to be a continuation of the phenomena that once centred around film-stars. A very strong group feeling is built up around a central figure, not entirely fictional, whose coat may be torn and hair disarrayed by fans. Often, such a figure, like Presley the ex-truck-driver, has lived for a time the kind of life the admirers know. But he will have triumphed to an extent unprecedented, both in terms of fame and finance. The followers are drawn with him into a new and exciting world. At this point the business men are involved with the chain of processes already described, to select and transmit the material that will be the most effective for the audiences. Even so there are limits as to how far these people can push fashion unless what they are trying to sell has some real significance for the customer and his needs. It has been suggested[8] that teenagers basically create their own idols but lose them when they become national figures, and for this reason turn to new gods.

There is a sense in which the triumph of the teenager in the world at large has become somewhat more than vicarious, through the fame of a chosen few. In America vast efforts are made to meet the younger people on their own ground. Record sales have shown that after the first fun of cheap 'singles', another peak is reached some months later because of demand for the same songs in the collected and more expensive form of the L.P. record. This is largely due to the adults who try to keep up with their offspring in this sort of way. Fashions in clothes tend to follow the same pattern. The father wears the clothes that once were the exclusive property of his fashionable

[8] *Observer*, November 10th, 1963.

son.[9] Clearly there is both promise and danger here. There can be little value in the extension of the peer-group to include parents and everyone else, since such a situation takes away the very credentials of the exclusive world into which the adolescent can learn in semi-private his new role in the community.

On the other hand, there can be great value in not having too rigid a division between the various cultural groups, so that, when the time comes, transference from one to another may take place. Of one thing we may be certain. Growing things need some shelter from the elements, the spirit of a teenager no less than the body of a baby. It is worth while to examine in a little more detail the elements on which such protective groupings are founded.

Group Solidarity

As far as popular music is concerned, the appeal to the need for group solidarity begins when record sales begin to rise into significant figures. The flood of publications and comment on the radio and television and in print about performers, along with mutual admiration and discussion amongst friends, contributes to the feeling of fellowship around a central enthusiasm. From time to time excitement centres on one particular performing group. In some ways a group of singers is better than an individual performer for this purpose. The smaller group reflects to some degree the larger group of followers, and there is a greater possibility that at least one of the idols may be similar in some way to particular individuals in his audience, thus making identification easier. If there is to be a 'live' concert, excitement is heightened by direct physical contact in a pushing, jostling queue for tickets. Even at this stage, before ever the performers are within ear-shot, shop-windows have been broken and semi-riotous situations reported by the police. On such occasions many young people realise for the first time

[9] G. and F. M. Hechinger, *Teenage Tyranny.*

the actuality of the numbers involved; not as a matter of statistics, but of actually being part of a great crowd. At the performance itself this experience becomes intense. Screaming becomes deafening and obliterates the sound of the music, until the performers want to shout back with John Lennon, 'Shurrup!' Most of this excitement is only possible because of the work put in to arouse and clarify the need to belong to a sympathetic group by those who manage the business affairs of the performers. When they actually appear in flesh and blood and the audience work upon each other by sheer noise and physical contact, no wonder the tension explodes into ecstasy. For some, hysteria and collapse, what some emotional religious sects call 'wiping the slate clean'; for others, release of all muscular control, including that of the bladder, and for a few, disappointment at not being able to hear the music: these are the ultimate symptoms and signs of behaviour within a group framework. Even without a concert as a focal point, the 'charts', that great unifying element, help to plot the progress of the idols and fix the attention of the worshippers. Many record shops report teenagers asking for the record at the top, without even knowing what it is called and who is performing it. They do not, they dare not, remain in ignorance for long.

Group Status

It is not enough merely to belong to a group: the group must have status of one sort or another. We all like to think that societies of which we happen to be a member are looked upon with respect from the outside world. This is natural enough because not only does 'belonging' satisfy our need for security, but it also is an extension of ourselves, and we share in the fortunes of the organisation. Reading through the literature that is widely distributed among the young – magazines and popular newspapers – one is impressed by the amount of detail about the wealth and success of popular stars. One journal analysed for its readers the secrets of seven popular groups under the following headings: Members; Birthplaces; Label A & R Man; Personal Manager; Agent; Big Break; First Hit; Where and When Formed; How Named; Equipment (often priced at over £4000); Influences; Favourite Work; Where Group Can Be Contacted. Not much of this is personal, even less is musical, and the impression is of a well-managed success story with a clear picture of the road to the top. In the more 'chatty' articles, details, such as the number of pairs of socks owned by Ringo, are tossed around with great authority as if the writer were personally familiar with every material possession of the singer. During a television programme when the Beatles 'took off' the Pyramus–Thisbe scene in *A Midsummer Night's Dream*, Ringo assured the audience that he was not really a lion at all; indeed, he said, if he were he would not be earning all the money that he was paid for being Ringo. The remark went down well. At a time of life when awkwardness and social failure often loom large, the status appeal of a successful teenager is extremely powerful. Success at something matters more to many youngsters than mere personal charm, and certainly more than sheer musical quality.

> The four command a kingdom of gold and silver trophies. They rule supreme from the hit parade heights. They dominate the thoughts, moods and hearts of a million devoted fans. They fascinate many more millions of longer-range admirers from every walk of life and every living generation.[10]

This is powerful stuff for those between childhood and adulthood, with its fairytale kingdoms on the one hand, the respect of *all* generations on the other, and the domination of hearts in the fairly near future. And what a pipe-dream is the description of Ringo, who has grown from 'a sad-faced urchin, scrounging empty boxes, to a confident, well balanced near millionaire, watched over and well loved by everyone'. For the maximum appeal he has to be both secure in the admira-

[10] From a record sleeve.

tion of the group and at the same time have the status of fame and hard cash.

Erotic Experience

The third powerful appeal is without doubt to the growing erotic feelings of the adolescent. On this level the words and the music, as we have seen, come into their own a little more. Whenever music is coupled with dancing there is nearly always some erotic significance, whether it be in the dance-hall, on the village green or at the ballet. The most striking feature of much dancing to recent pop music is the phenomenon of separate and isolated dancing with only vague reference to a partner. This may well be a fairly natural and tentative first step for the sexually inexperienced, a reluctance to leave the shelter of the herd and take up life with a female. Sometimes the music itself has a more than usual erotic effect. 'The music seems to build up to a climax and you feel like shouting' said one boy. It is important to realise that most of the sensuality embodied in pop music is exploratory rather than ultimately satisfying. The youngster is finding his or her way about through a maze of new and often intense feelings, and it is no cause for surprise if, at first, the balance appears to be lop-sided. For example, the long hair and slightly female appearance of many popular groups has added to their attraction for younger girls. In the same kind of way that 'crushes' are formed for an older girl or boy or a teacher of the same sex, so it is both exciting and safe to surrender to a soft-faced young man at one remove. Yet some relief of frustrated feeling is available. 'God! it's the greatest catharsis I've ever had', said a girl to her friends as they left Carnegie Hall.[11]

To demonstrate clearly the relative importance of the musical and cultural elements in popular song, we only need a crude analysis to indicate where it is that the power lies. We

[11] Mentioned by M. Braun, *The Beatles' Progress*.

have already looked briefly at *Bits and Pieces* and we could summarise its musical virtues thus:

Melodically – A limited range, easy to sing, has the blues 'third' now and then to provide a slightly doleful sound.

Rhythmically – A simple, plodding pulse with an unsyncopated top-line, yielding practically no feeling of 'swing'.

Harmonically – A plagal cadence, "Amen" thirty-two times.

Vocally – Strained but fairly cheerful noise, much amplified.

Instrumentally – Guitar and percussion provide a fairly stimulating 'backing', but the excitement tends to be proportionate to the volume.

Verbally – Belongs to the lost-love variety, but the emphasis seems to be on the cheerful fact of ever having a love at all.

General effect – Cheerful noise, moderately stimulating, quite good to dance to and an easy tune to whistle or sing.

A run-down of its *cultural* significance would be quite different:

Group solidarity – Millions of people of the same age and inclinations are focusing attention on to the performers. Parents may be hostile or indifferent but those who care are together, unified in buying the records, reading the relevant literature and sharing admiration with each other.

Group status – The singers, roughly the same age as the listeners, at least in *appearance and behaviour*, are socially adored, professionally recognised and financially very comfortable indeed. It is easy to share by proxy these coveted things.

Erotic experience – (Girls) Performers are usually distinctive-looking boys who often sing of love. This can be enjoyed in safety and in fantasy without the difficulties of actual relationships, and without the unknown dangers that attend sexual behaviour. (Boys) It is possible to be adored in the same way as the performers, and they can easily become a safe substitute for real relationships or possibly be imitated with similar results. We might notice that girls and boys play a different role. The former are the most violent in their behaviour, whilst the latter go ahead and learn to play the guitar.

General effect – Powerful romantic and erotic feelings are given some encouragement, but at the same time there is an almost tangible feeling of security in belonging to the larger group of admirers. The music all helps it to grow in pressure but can ultimately be shouted down at the climax and paroxysm of the concert performance.

Exploitation

In the light of all this we must consider the extent and the dangers of exploitation of teenagers by certain sections of the business world. There can be no doubt that popular music is the centre of a large and flourishing industry and that, as in most large selling operations, there is a fair amount of pressure, applied somctimes dishonestly, upon those who might buy. Even one of our most respected encyclopedias has recently come under criticism of the way in which it was being retailed. We must not jump to the conclusion that just because it is possible to exploit people by the sale of a certain commodity that the article is, *ipso facto*, corrupt in itself. When musical sounds are put together to make a pop tune it is possible to use the result in more than one way, depending on the attitudes and beliefs of the customers. It may be true that those who sell are in a position of being able to influence, to some extent, the wishes of those who buy. But it must be remembered that the product in the first place is not a creation, but an *extension* of a need which must have foundations in real desires and actual feelings. 'What the masses get is but the reflection of their own vociferous needs and demands.'[12] The most highly paid musicians today are those who are able to hold a mirror to the emotions of the audience. The music can be more than this, and

[12] Brown, *op. cit.*

some of it is, but for the vast majority the piece is a signal, telling the customer which role he must play for the sake of satisfaction and security. This complex sign-language is emotionally charged and a better term for it might be a *slogan*. When pop music is used as a slogan the teenager is handed back in clear and unmistakable terms an answer to his own needs for simple and safe emotive experience. The same advantages and dangers are present as with a verbal slogan: they are useful in simplifying issues, in encouraging action, and in promoting social unity, but they can be coined before the truth is really known, and shouted when no longer relevant. Slogans teach us nothing, they simply reinforce what we would like to believe. 'Pop is rubbish!' is no more valuable than 'The Stones are great'. We have seen, though, that the adolescent is grateful for the security which such slogans provide. He needs a feeling of 'oneness' with his peers, and some clear motivation to action when beset by complex and painful personal situations, by contradictory thoughts and feelings. The simplification of slogan making and slogan-chanting is sometimes, and for short spells, useful. Even so, there are dangers.

A great deal of commercial energy is expended in informing teenagers of the trends and fashions that attend pop music.[13] Fair enough, but the question comes to mind as to the amount of genuine *feed-back* from the adolescent community to the industry, as compared with the *manufacture* of trends by the commercial people. A clear example is found in a comparison of the spread of 'rock 'n roll' with the rise of the 'twist'. The former caught on almost by accident in this country and no one was prepared for the enthusiasm with which it was taken up. The 'twist', on the other hand, came as close to the invention of a trend as it is possible to get. Advertising gimmicks and the 'hard sell' were in evidence before teenagers had really heard any music at all. More recently the Monkees were built up into a group by the

---

[13] This aspect has been well described by Connie Alderson in *Magazines Teenagers Read*: Pergamon, 1967.

business world and put over on television. This is quite different from the rise into fame of an *existing* amateur group like the Beatles and many others. Some TV programmes have attempted to build atmosphere around pop stars for an audience of 8- to 10-year-olds, though the general impression is of indifference on the part of the children (*Five O'Clock Club*, for example). A small girl on a radio programme said that she liked the music of Bach and Beethoven, but that she thought herself not yet old enough to appreciate the Beatles! Would that all young children were as wise and honest. Attempts to force slogans down the throats of unbelievers are always to be deplored.

Just as it is unnecessary to treat small children as adolescents, so there must be provision at the other end of the teenage tunnel to turn to other things. It is at this point that the responsibility lies to a great extent with the teacher, for he sees the beginning and often the end of the need for the solace that pop can offer to his pupils. He has to understand the ways in which such music is used by the children and direct attention to the best possible, the most fruitful usage. The greatest weakness of pop music in general is in the froth and bubble that gathers about it. Only by taking time and trouble to examine what lies beneath can the foam be dispelled. It remains now to investigate the ways in which pop music appears to impinge in the classroom on the teacher's work and aims.

The Cult and the Classroom

To what extent does this music interfere with the work of the teacher? What are the principle factors which cause the situation? We have already answered in part the second of these questions: the most powerful elements of popular music are those which can be designated 'cultural' rather than 'artistic'. However, it is both interesting and useful to observe and take part in situations in the classroom where these pressures are clearly demonstrated. For this reason, the writer conducted a series of experiments which will only be described here in the briefest way.

The first step was to devise a musical thermometer to gauge, at least in the short term, the temperature of appreciation of various kinds of music. Actually, what can be measured tends to be the degree of *willingness to listen*. Teachers feel that the problem is not that children are unable to understand something of the music presented in different ways to them, but rather that 'they are just not interested'. What we really want to know is the degree and the nature of interest in 'teacher's music' in the face of the popular challenger. After a great deal of discussion with teachers and pupils a ten-point scale evolved which was devised to run from high pleasure to a complete failure to find either interest or enjoyment. The more emotional terms are mixed with the more intellectual words, since it was found that some children 'feel' their way through the music while others find it 'interesting'. The final scale ran as follows:

1. Very Exciting	6. Quite Interesting
2. Exciting	7. Acceptable
3. Absorbing	8. Endurable
4. Enjoyable	9. Dull
5. Pleasing	10. Dead Boring

It can be objected that these terms mean different things to different people and that some of the words are too difficult. However, in the grammar school in which they were first used, no one felt the order to be wrong, which is the main thing, and later, when the tests were made amongst children of lower ability, they were asked simply to mark what they heard out of ten. Several trials were carried out and it was found that both of these systems were satisfactory when used as described below.

This scale, once it was found to be practicable, was put into use, first to establish reactions to a piece of music normally associated. with the classroom, and then to check reactions after some degree of conditioning by popular music. In other words, a comparison was to be made between scores on the same piece of classical music before and after the changes of atmosphere caused by popular music. It is the classical piece that is having the attention and not the other material. The choice of such a 'test-piece' was important, for it had to have clear associations with 'school music', it had to be 'square'. Music with extra-musical associations, such as opera, incidental music, programme music and so on, was avoided, and so also were pieces with strong dramatic, tragic or violently self-assertive qualities. A natural choice seemed to be a Haydn rondo, and, in fact, the last movement from Symphony Number 104 was chosen. The movement has humour and shape, grace and good manners; it is lively and yet has moments of quiet tenderness. Anyone capable of a high degree of appreciation might well find it exciting, but for others it could be boring.

To begin with, this movement was played to groups of children on two occasions a week apart. They gave a score on the ten-point scale and there was no significant change in scores between the two playings. Then this was repeated with four other groups of 14-year-olds, A, B, C, D, streamed according to academic ability. Before the second playing, with this experimental group, for between fifteen to twenty minutes, popular songs were played on the gramophone. They were pieces that the children wanted to hear and in fact they lent the material to the teacher. The songs were: *The Rise and Fall of Flingel Bunt* (Shadows); *You're No Good* (Swinging Blue Jeans); *The House of the Rising Sun* (The Animals); *It's All Over Now* (The Rolling Stones). All of these could be classified as jazz-derived pop tunes. The results were significant. On average, those children of high academic ability found the Haydn movement slightly more enjoyable the second time, in spite of the popular music played beforehand. Those in the lowest stream, on the other hand, scored on average two points lower down the scale. A similar pattern emerged when the groups were considered from the point of view of their stated musical preferences. Those who liked classical music to begin with were able to enjoy the second playing more, while those who put pop and jazz before classical in order of preference lost the liking that they had to some extent when forced to hear both kinds of music side by side. In general it was found that those children with high ability *and* a predisposition towards classical music gained, on average, 10 per cent more enthusiasm for the classical piece, as measured by the ten-point scale, while those in the bottom stream *without* any liking for classical music dropped 25 per cent. The other groups came in between, giving a mathematically good graph, thus indicating the validity of both the scale and the method. This whole experiment was repeated by a different person in a secondary modern school with just the same results. We can say quite firmly that about three-quarters of our adolescents in school are less willing to listen to classical music because of the existence of popular music as we know it at present. We can also say that the other quarter are able, to some degree or other, not only to resist these effects, but actually to find classical music *more* satisfying in comparison with the particular sort of popular pieces played in this experiment.

A similar set of tests with different groups of 14-year-olds was carried out, but instead of using popular music as the conditioning element *jazz* was played. Musically speaking, as we have seen, jazz is more virile and sensational than most of its popular imitations. Jazz, as such, is not at all popular with school children of any age. There were a few children (4 per cent) who put jazz down as their first preference but a large number said they liked it not at all. The result of this experiment indicated that only those few who really believed in the potency of jazz lost any liking for the classical piece that was played afterwards. The jazz pieces included the following:

Papa Dip (New Orleans Wanderers, 1926); *Potato Head Blues* (Armstrong, 1927); *Jazz Me Blues* (Beiderbecke, 1927); *Buddy Bolden Stomp* (Bechet, 1948). The classical piece was the last movement of Haydn's Symphony Number 94. Those with a real liking for jazz found the classical piece far less likeable when it was juxtaposed with jazz than it was when considered during the course of more orthodox music lessons, but the vast majority were influenced neither way, no matter what the level of ability. The lesson seems clear: we only find disturbingly strong results if the pupils believe in the creed that the music signifies. Our problem is a *cultural* one at rock-bottom, not merely an issue of relatively simple musical preferences.

We know that popular music can interfere with the work that many music teachers are trying to do. We know that this is related to ability and to musical background and preferences. We also know that the most powerful forces at work are those to do with adolescence as a sub-culture. What remains is to look at the teacher's position in this cultural and social set-up, to discuss some of the deep-rooted problems that lie, like a chasm, between the world of teacher and pupil.

A great deal of what has been said so far may appear obvious to some readers but at least an attempt has been made to set the record straight on some of the issues involved, and having done this we are better equipped to indicate with more confidence appropriate remedial measures.

CHAPTER 5

CULTURE AND THE TEACHER

"We remarked with pain that the indecent foreign dance called the *Waltz* was introduced (we believe for the first time) at the English Court on Friday last. This is a circumstance which ought not to be passed over in silence. National morals depend on national habits: and it is quite sufficient to cast one's eyes on the voluptuous intertwining of the limbs, and close compressure on the bodies, in their dance, to see that it is indeed far removed from the modest reserve which has hitherto been considered distinctive of English females. So long as this obscene display was confined to prostitutes and adulteresses, we did not think it deserving of notice: but now it is attempted to be forced on the respectable classes of society by the evil example of their superiors, we feel it a duty to warn every parent against exposing his daughter to so fatal a contagion. *Amicus Plato sed Atagis veritas.* We pay due deference to our superiors in rank, but we owe a higher duty to morality. We know not how it happened (probably the recommendation of some worthless and ignorant dancing master) that so indecent a dance has now for the first time been exhibited at the English Court; but the novelty is one deserving of severe reprobation, and we trust it will never again be tolerated in any moral English society."

(*The Times*, July 16th, 1816)

IF POPULAR music arouses and stimulates strong feelings in young people, it is also true that it provokes older folk to a strong reaction of one sort or another. Paul Johnson of the *New Statesman* has complained bitterly about the 'intellectual treachery' of those who should know better, but who, in fact praise the Beatles. (The message was aimed in particular at Mr. Deedes, then a cabinet minister.) He comments on the young people who can be seen on television pop music programmes as part of the audience.

What a bottomless chasm of vacuity they reveal! The huge faces, bloated with cheap confectionery and smeared with chain-store make-up, the open, sagging mouths, the hands mindlessly drumming in time to the music, the broken stiletto heels, the shoddy, stereotyped, 'with-it' clothes: Here apparently is a collective portrait of a generation enslaved by a commercial machine.[1]

Many letters were written in answering sally to this attack. In two weeks the paper received 170 letters criticising Mr. Johnson, 66 supporting him and a number of 'neutrals'. David Holbrook wrote saying that 'twist and shout' really means 'copulate and cry out', and dealt with pop music in terms of 'masturbation fantasies'. To this Deryck Cooke replied:

that he is simply affected by puritanical disgust in the face of those sexually evocative movements which form a natural and healthy part of a great deal of the world's dancing, whether folk or pop. This impression is confirmed by his curious phrase 'a low kind of masturbation'. Is there then a 'high' kind of masturbation?

Impassioned comment and criticism of the music and dancing of young people breaks out in the press, and in less ephemeral media from time to time. The waltz was considered 'indecent' at the beginning of the last century, jazz represented 'immorality' at the beginning of this century, and popular music has been seen more recently to be a symptom of 'perversion'. The interesting thing is that those who spoke against jazz often adored the waltz, and that the strongest critics of pop music are often jazz enthusiasts. There is no need to duplicate examples of the heated discussion that broke out during the height of 'Beatlemania' in 1963–4. Fan and anti-fan letters filled local and national papers whenever the Beatles were in town; for it was the Beatles who brought the matter to its most recent climax both in terms of music and of culture. Jazz musicians grumbled, academics took up causes and waved the flag, and teachers and educationalists muttered vague platitudes. The most alarming feature is the state of indecision that seems to exist among teachers and those who

[1] *New Statesman*, February 28th, 1964.

give them advice, even when confronted by such violent manifestations. The truth is that we like to let sleeping dogs lie, and so remain totally unprepared when the animal springs into life. In a publication brought out in 1964,[2] offering help to teachers of music, popular music is given no serious attention at all. One contributer suggests that each individual teacher must decide for himself. Another sees the issue in simple black and white: 'Classical and Popular music represent an antithesis only as music for serious listening, and music for background or negligible concentration.' Some individuals with interest in music-teaching have gone so far as to say that there is really no problem, and that we should just plough on ignoring all but the music we like ourselves.

To help to form a clearer picture all secondary school music teachers in a large midland town were sent a questionnaire. Only ten replied. One of these ten used pop in the classroom 'quite often'; six played it as 'light relief' occasionally, and three teachers never played it at all. Of these three, two felt that this type of music hindered appreciation of classical works, and two of the six who played it occasionally felt that it had effects of this sort. The single person who used pop quite often would not generalise.

> With girls (particularly lower intelligence groups) I think it is a hindrance – they tend to become swamped by pop and it is difficult to open their minds to other music. We try to avoid: classics good, pop bad, etc. Rather: there are good classics, bad classics, good pops bad pops.

Six of the ten teachers found a little personal pleasure in popular music, some of it at any rate, while the other four found none at all. 'Though I enjoy *every* other kind of music current pop music I find boring in its crudity.' One teacher in a boys' grammar school made his position clear. 'I have no wish to encourage bad taste, ugly noise, both instrumental and vocal; bowdlerised versions of classical tunes; artificially

[2] *Handbook for Music Teachers*, Ed. Rainbow.

Americanised use of English.' Another complained that the third-year pupils seemed the worst affected group, while yet another noted even in the second year at school a tendency to find the song-book 'silly', and to prefer the more 'erotic' songs they hear on the Light Programme. What were the opinions of the other twenty teachers in the town we shall never know, but the odds are that they were either not interested or were irritated by the whole topic. At any rate thay can hardly have been enthusiastic about the possibilities of using pop music in the classroom.

There are many ways of presenting the arguments for and against popular music, but we must now turn to the central issues without becoming either abusive or emotional. Mr. Gillies[3] answers nicely the suggestion, that pop is a point of departure for the adolescent, by saying that most teachers 'know instinctively that its point is limited and its departure doubtful'. Richard Hoggart[4] has perhaps given the clearest and fairest indictment against the more trivial popular entertainments in saying 'it is not that they prevent their readers from becoming highbrow, but that they make it harder for people without any intellectual bent to become wise in their own way'.

One answer to the growing threat of such an inadequate pop culture, as so many consider it to be, is to train the citizen 'to discriminate and to resist'.[5] H. L. Wilensky,[6] engaged on a project showing that only the very unusual person in America can avoid mass culture, concludes that we need to invest heavily in those institutions which 'aggressively uphold cultural standards'. Only in this way can we prevent a decline in high culture. In the same manner, only more specifically, Ivor Keys,[7] speaking to delegates of the Schools' Music Association

[3] Article in the *Musical Times*, September 1964.
[4] *The Uses of Literacy.*
[5] Leavis in *Culture and Environment*, Chatto, 1942.
[6] Article in *New Society*, May 14th, 1964.
[7] Reported in *The Times Educational Supplement*, November 6th, 1964.

insists: 'Let us be square and say so – otherwise there won't be anything square left. We must mount a persistent attack against the purveyance of the second rate.'

These sort of views reflect one side of the case, and with many of the points we must agree. The crux of the issue seems to be in the question of where the second rate is to be found, and how it can be eliminated. Closely allied to this is the difficulty of establishing an acceptable body of criticism and evaluation, which will help to define 'good' and 'bad' in artistic terms, and distinguish the first-rate from the poor. There are two dangers to be avoided. On the one hand, to proclaim popular music as the folk-music of our time, worthy of our attention and respect, is to risk forgetting the fact that only the very best folk-music has survived from the past and that, no doubt, a good deal of what passed for folk-music was second rate by any standards. On the other hand, to recommend 'aggressive' resistance to mass culture is to risk embracing a set of standards imposed by a cultured minority, and these standards may well be based on an historical, museum tradition. The discussion that takes place between one view and another, that is, the argument for and against the artistic validity of pop music and its place in education, reduces itself eventually to a proper understanding of the ways in which we use the word 'culture'. In this very paragraph the word has been used with two distinct meanings. We speak of 'mass culture' and 'a cultured minority'.

The Meaning of 'Culture'

The first use of this term stems from the idea of culture as 'a way of life'.[8] Owen, Ruskin and Morris, and more recently D. H. Lawrence and Leavis, have all helped to develop this notion of culture *growing* 'organically' out of the community. T. S. Eliot has defined British culture as 'the pintable, the dartboard, Wensleydale cheese, boiled cabbage cut into sections,

[8] This is discussed very fully in *Culture and Society*, by Raymond Williams.

and the music of Elgar'. Culture is, in other words, the total picture of the organisation of society, from the board-room, or the way in which the roads are swept, to the symphony concert. The fine arts are only a part of this, just one manifestation of man imposing order and shape on his environment. Sociologists tend to use the word culture to describe 'all behavioural patterns and their formations'. In this definition, ultimately, culture is equated with civilisation or organisation.

The definition has changed gradually out of all recognition in the hands of those who seek to extend the range of 'taste' for commercial reasons, and the crudest contemporary rendering is simply that the greatest happiness of the greatest number is the only justification for art. The line of modification runs like this: Organic development is good, mechanical and contrived change is bad; the organs of society are the social groups and the largest group should have the right to control; interference with 'natural' development is bad; a cultural minority constitutes a threat of interference in that it may want to 'educate' or censor; therefore an élite is undesirable and mass culture is the ultimate, since it represents more nearly the wishes and feelings of the bulk of the population. The validity of this reasoning rests upon the assumption that society exists and develops without internal or external pressures, interference, or persuasion of any sort, which is nonsense. Yet such assumptions are present in some degree when a business man says, 'I only sell what people want, I don't have to persuade them', and when a schoolboy avers, 'most people like it so it must be good'.

The fact is that 'liking' and 'wanting', whether it be soap-powder or music, can, and to some degree *are* being *created* by powerful organisations with all the sophisticated techniques of market-research and advertising at their disposal. Fortunately there are limits, but even so these can be pushed further and further, as the customer is educated and initiated into wanting streamlined versions of his own feedback. In short, culture as a 'way of life' has been perverted, in the course of time, and because of the potency of the mass-media, into culture of the masses, implying an artificially stimulated set of needs, wants and standards. It is this pervading attitude that has made possible the confrontation between 'high-brow' and 'low-brow'; between classical and popular music; between the teacher and his pupils.

The alternative definition of 'culture' can be traced back to the Romantic artists and writers of the last century. Wordsworth, for example, saw the poet as a 'rock of defence for human nature'. Later, Carlyle saw a need for men concerned with the *quality* of life, and Arnold postulated the group of 'aliens', who would shape and lead to some extent the rest of the community. In this century, Shaw conceived of a 'remnant' (the Fabians), an intellectual aristocracy. At present we hear a lot about 'academics' and a 'literary minority'. The idea goes back certainly to antiquity. The 'clerisy' of Coleridge, the 'aliens' of Arnold and the 'remnant' of Shaw, are the 'philosopher-kings' of Plato, minus their kingdoms and most of their powers. They are reduced to infiltrating through the medium of art into the invisible world of the soul. In fact, this classical version of Pooh Bah was never a reality in Plato's time, still less so now. Philosopher is separated from King; King is excommunicated from the Church and the Priest divorced from the State; the Artist finds no function for his vision in the community at large; and the literary minority cannot make contact with the man in the street. So much for culture as 'the finer things of life'.

Here we have two alternatives, or so it seems at first. Either we accept the doctrine of mass culture, with its built-in notion of the survival of the fittest, or we join ranks with the élite and exist in a world that is viewed from outside with a curious mixture of respect and ridicule. It tends to be the world of the 'serious' artist, musician and writer, the realm of the 'academic' in university, college and school. During this century so far we have, as a community, tended to remove ourselves out of the control of the few and into the power of the many. We have managed to jump out of the proverbial frying-pan, dominated by aristocracy and meritocracy, into the fire of the ad.-man.

The solution is not to revert to a simple, medieval type of existence, even if this were possible. In some way standards must grow out through the community in an organic fashion, and yet still be more than just a reflection or aggravation of what Lord Hailsham called, the 'highest common factor of endurance without enthusiasm'. Just as it is hard for the 'ordinary' person to come to terms with the ideas and thoughts of the élite, so it is also hard for the critics of mass culture to have real contact and understanding with the people of whom they write. They may be able to make detailed observations of a certain kind, but they lack empathy with those whose lives they view from the outside. This is the centre of the problem of popular music, or any sort of popular manifestation or expression. The means of achieving the intimate experience, of living the feelings of the many, whilst at the same time preserving objective judgement and high standards: this is the great need of our times. As far as pop music is concerned the issue is not, on the one hand, that the 'low' musician is a weakness in terms of the 'high' musician, nor, on the other hand, is it that every serious musician has no desire to be understood by a wider audience. The issue is that the worlds of 'low' and 'high' are divided, both in function and material and in the groups of people that tend to patronise them respectively. Our problem is not so much dilution, or corruption, but *separation*, which allows and encourages the misuse and watering-down of popular music as well as the perpetuation of obscurity that attends much so-called serious art.

In some way, culture – 'a way of life' has to find reference to culture – 'the quality of life'. The artist and writer, the intellectual and the musician, must become aware of and responsive to the simpler reflective, expressive qualities of society.

The pulse of the way of life needs to be continually felt, and if the artist will not attend to the symbolic needs of the community then the business man will. At the same time, we need as a community a certain amount of detachment and a sense of direction, so that new things may emerge in the sciences and the arts, without the fettering caused by pressing demands of immediate problems, and lack of funds for something that may appear on the surface to have no use. On the one hand we must avoid the petrifaction of that which 'has no place for the off-beat until it is safely buried and can be treated as a museum piece',[9] and 'exploitation of the cheapest emotional response'[10] on the other. The common ground is not educational attainment, nor is it level of wealth, nor is it intellectual equality: it is surely *human feeling*, not just as it is felt but as it is presented in relationships with other people, in humour and in art. This is what makes the role of the teacher of art subjects in our schools so vital and why a failure to cope with popular music and its effects is so serious. The musician has, by the very nature of his 'subject', one of the most effective unifying elements that exists.

Some readers may well be wondering whether this diversion into the problems of 'culture' has been really necessary. The answer is – no – unless we really want to understand what pop music is all about. For it exists only as part of a larger pattern and it can only be properly described with reference to that pattern. The tension between pop and other music is only a part of a whole area of bad communications. It happens to be that part where the divisions and failures are most exposed to view. The music teacher is handling material that for him, as a member of the cultural élite, has musical significance. His pupils, as we have seen in a previous chapter, will tend to understand this material of musical sound in terms of their culture, or adolescent way of life. The friction between these

[9] K. W. Richmond, *Culture and General Education.*
[10] *Culture and Environment.*

concepts is made worse because the music in use is so often not even of this century. There is nothing wrong with this, of course, but it does seem to children rather strange when, after reading modern verse in English, or painting an abstract in the Art room, they come to a music lesson and spend most of it singing *Fairest Isle* or listening to the music of a composer who died 150 years ago.

There is another reason too which we should honestly take into account. For some musicians, and especially those who find their way into some of our schools, music is a form of escape. If we really examine our motives for being what we are we might find that, at some stage or other, music became a *need* and a place of withdrawal. This is a part, but only part of the function of music. It is not difficult to find people who have retreated to the organ-loft, or to the pit of the opera-house, or to composition in some form or other, or into music-teaching because of some basic inability to face up to the reality of life. There are many teachers and musicians who are outward-going and flexible, but there are others who are permanently immersed in a limited range of music for reasons of personal, mental and emotional security. In other words, they are using their music in a similar kind of way to that of the pop-possessed adolescent. The result can only be terrible strain and friction, for both parties are trying to preserve what the other is trying to destroy. The teacher feels that all that he holds sacred is being trampled under foot, and the pupil feels no less affronted by what appears to be an attempt to undermine his *credo*. Music divides where it should unite, and in its division reflects and exaggerates the divisions of society. A closer look at the musical sub-structures that seem to exist at present will help towards a positive approach to the dilemma.

The Pattern of our Musics

It is possible to distinguish many musical genres beyond merely classical, jazz or pop. There are two extremes to the pattern made by our many musics at present. The most formal and least expressive extreme is the music produced in a random, mechanical or electronic way, when human feeling and control is eliminated as far as possible. 'Musique concrète' is an example, where many different and complex sounds are scrambled electronically. This sort of music is a logical result of the aesthetic beliefs of Stravinsky and Hindemith and a natural successor to the concentrated compositions of Webern and Berg. The ultimate result is pattern without obvious feeling, except, at times, the 'emotion of avoiding the emotions'. The other extreme has been called 'beat', meaning in this case those elements of jazz, and modern jazz especially, considered by some existentialist intellectuals to be worthy of attention. The emphasis is on involvement of feelings without organisation, and the lives of the devotees often follow a similar anti-pattern. In either of these positions there is little contact with the community at large, unless, as sometimes happens, the sounds produced in the 'laboratory' are used for documentary films, and the throb of the beat in the 'pad' be laid on for dancing or making love.[11]

These extremes reflect the cultural extremes of our society, for one seeks to impose order via the intellect while the other tries to find a vague Nirvana, using music as a kind of drug. But we have seen that the musician is concerned neither with chance, chaotic feelings nor mere construction and elaboration of sound-patterns. If he is to play a role in society he must avoid the sterile division between aimless self-expression and the academic detachment that can trace patterns, and find 'trends', without ever knowing the forces of human feeling that must be part of the account. The creative artist 'is neither priest nor slave, but a member of society to whom is entrusted certain qualities essential to the intellectual and social life of society'.[12]

[11] See L. Lipton, *The Holy Barbarians*, for a description of the "beat" generation.
[12] A. Silbermann, *The Sociology of Music*.

Both the extremes have their counterpart among the mentally sick. On the one hand is the patient who alternates between elation and depression, his intellect at the mercy of his emotive condition. His problem is that of *unpatterned feeling*. The paranoid or catatonic patient, on the other hand, seems to know nothing of hate, fear or love, but sits in a tight bundle, shut up within himself, repeating over and over again the same motive in speech, drawing, or bodily action. His is the state of *patterned unfeeling*. Both patients are ill. The enormity of reducing music to shapeless sensation is no better or worse than reducing it to sensationless shape. Yet the latter is what many composers have achieved in the first half of this century, and the former is daily evident in so much popular music.

It is perhaps no mere coincidence that the devotees of experimental music and 'beat' are often similar in appearance. The beard and sandals and the style of life are the hallmarks of the 'way out'. For one set, nonconformity has produced its own rules and mores; for the other there exists a feeling that feelings are dangerous. Essentially, both are withdrawn from the main ways of our society, and are to some degree in retreat from the uncertainties of the modern community, and from burdens which modern communications have laid on us all. The esoteric musician and the hippies looking for a psychedelic experience through drugs and drug-like music are both in need of orientation within the community and within themselves. There is a sense in which the music of both worlds may be usefully experimental, evolving techniques which may later on become part of a living tradition. At any given time and under their own power though, these extremes are just not viable. At least neither genre can be accused of merely pandering to popular demand, since one side eschews feeling altogether and the other seeks out only certain special sensations. These, in theory, are the present limits.

It is possible to trace a kind of descent from these opposite poles. The formal side, if we may call it so, would include the 'avant-garde' composer and his audience who, whilst avoiding the purely mechanical, tends, like Cage and Davidson, Cowell and Varèse, towards sound-pattern. Becoming more approachable as we leave the more extreme positions is a group of 'accepted' modern composers, including Britten, Tippett, Copland and Rawsthorne, who may be considered to be eclectic, breaking new ground while still using elements which provide a link with the past and the people. The next related stage of the journey down the formal side would be of listeners only, since the composers happen to be dead. The best concert certainties, from a box-office point of view, are still the Classical and Romantic composers, including Beethoven and Tchaikovsky in particular. More recently, as a reaction in part against the more formal extremes, Mahler and Bruckner have found their way into the standard repertoire. The next stage down is a derivation from this concert-hall fare, and could be called 'Light Classical'. Operetta, Strauss, Sullivan, Grieg and Balfe spring to mind. Some of the music of Mozart and 'Gems from Italian Opera' arranged for brass-band would come under this heading. The emphasis is on snippets, sewn together by arrangers and heard as an evocation of bygone days in 'Palm Court' hotels. The direction of travel is away from the experimental and intellectual towards the most acceptable to the greatest number of people. The diagram below summarises this description. In actual fact the various musics shade off imperceptibly into each other.

A similar line of progression may be traced from 'beat' (meaning the more specialised and esoteric kind of jazz-derived music) to the mainstreams of jazz, both traditional and modern. The great variety of styles – from the M.J.Q. to Armstrong – is a similar example of musical selectivity to that of avant-garde composers on the formal side. Pop music at its most potent is derived from jazz, though some of it filters in from the classical side. Dance music is a strange mixture of pop, jazz and even musical-comedy tunes and older waltzes.

It seems to utilise odd fragments of expressive music, just as 'light classical' borrows trinkets from the store of formal composers. Modern musical comedy is sometimes close to operetta, but it often borrows the 'beat' and vocabulary of jazz.

Between the derivations of the formal and expressive is the amorphous mass of 'light' music, where anything goes, providing it does not make either formal or expressive demands on the listener. A fair amount of military and brass-band music,

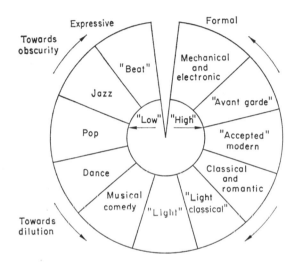

some 'old tyme' dance pieces, many film scores and cheerful marches written in the style of Elgar: all tend towards this division. It includes Mantovani, smoothing down the classics and Liberace, 'condensing' for his audience and, worst of all, so many items on publishers' lists designed for schools. 'Educational music' certainly helps to keep the writers of musical platitudes in business.

Even some of our very best music can be *used* by those who sell and by those who listen in this way. 'Light' music is never offensive, coarse, erotic or violent; neither is it noble, visionary, or in any real sense stirring or exciting. Vague patriotic or romantic feelings emerge and disappear. One meeting-ground for this borrowing, arranging, and diluting genre used to be the cinema-organ: now it is the soundtrack of some films, *Housewives' Choice*, and the supermarket. The medley emerges: sometimes old songs, sometimes jazz standards or bits of Beethoven, sometimes swung and sometimes straight but never too much of anything. A blues song is given a bank of wailing violins and a heavenly choir, and the 'high' and 'low' musics are united – in a pool of slush! It is here that we might well employ ourselves in rooting out the cliché, attacking the second rate and aggressively upholding standards. This way of using music, as a pastime, a background, or a mild sedative, becomes so easily a substitute for the vital, living flux of feelings that is presented in the best art and music. There is a danger that adolescents may grow no taller than the current pop tune or the weaker forms of jazz, but this danger is no greater than that demonstrated by the lady in middle-age who loves *All In The April Evening* but cannot enjoy a Bach cantata. The limitations for both are as restricting. It is true that the effects of 'light' music are not outwardly so strong or erotic – the group and status pressures are not so great – but the nostalgia and daydreams can be just as cramping to any real education of feeling. They may become a substitute for genuine emotion.

Before going any further we must be clear that when this sort of dilution takes place it is of something that was originally, and perhaps still is, wholesome and nourishing. A lot of pop is diluted jazz, 'Victorian' anthems are usually watered-down Mozart and Mendlessohn, while other forms of 'light' music collect their easy progressions from many sources. Not all of the actual musical material is poor. The diluting is, as often as not, perpetrated by the type of performance or by the audience. Here again we can say that the same musical piece can be an illuminating *symbol* of our emotional life or simply a *signal* for nostalgia, or sweet associations with pleasant things. This may be perfectly legitimate at times but it does not rank as a real musical experience, and the teacher should be sure that what he has to offer in the classroom is *living music*, and not just an evocation of his student days at the Academy or College. Otherwise his case is no better than that of his pupils. If he chooses Beethoven as part of his syllabus then he should do more than bring to it his own smaller feelings. Whether the genre is formal or expressive in emphasis, the reading-in of personal emotion, by composer, performer or listener, will destroy the artistic illusion and the ultimate significance of the work. We are reminded of Julia the actress, heart-broken over the infidelity of her lover.[13] She plays her own love and loss into the character on the stage and feels that she had never played so magnificently. But her husband tells her that her acting is *below* standard, and so she rests for a while, to return eventually to the part.

> She realized that all Michael had said was true. She took hold of herself. Thrusting her private emotion into the background and thus getting the character under control, she managed once more to play with her accustomed virtuosity. Her acting ceased to be a means by which she gave release to her feelings and was again the manifestation of her creative instinct. She got a quiet exhilaration out of thus recovering mastery over her medium. It gave her a sense of power and of liberation.

The intrusion of private emotion is the only thing left for the audience if what the composer, or performer, or those who present the music offer is insubstantial.

The model of musical genres is, of course, a very wide and crude generalisation, but it does help to keep the various factors in mind. It also makes the point that so many people tend to divide the diagram *vertically* – form being opposed to expression, minority set against the mass – whereas what we should do is to discriminate inside each subdivision. We shall probably

[13] Somerset Maugham, *Theatre*, pp. 145–9.

find that most really worthwhile music comes into a wide band across the middle of the diagram, though there can be value and stimulation in the upper reaches and healthy relaxation down at the bottom. Any unusual music (to our ears) such as oriental sounds and so on would be placed somewhere at the top, because of its obscurity for most people in the western world. We have already noted though that the new devices of one generation are the clichés of the next, and we should be prepared for mobility round the diagram. The important thing is to treat any description or model of musical culture as a flexible approximation, but to understand the significance of the extremes, and be aware of the general pattern.

Once we accept the fact that polarity of form and feeling is the life-blood of music, and reject the invitation to shout across from one side to another 'mass culture', or 'minority dictators', we can begin to assess the quality of individual pieces, no matter what the source. Music, by its very nature, is able to act as a bridge, a link between the instinctive and intellectual sides of each individual and the community. We need composers who are able to cross and recross the form-expression divide, and there are signs that this is happening. We need a sense of responsibility among those who represent the wider society as patrons and organisers of musical events: there seems to be hope here too. We also need teachers who are qualified to assist with the birth of a culture without splits or seams, where the *quality* of life is the *way* of life. Most teachers, because of their age and educational training, will need to come to terms with music very different from that in which they are immersed. We need to acquire sympathy with the best of expressive music, as well as with the standard works and the more forward-looking composers. If we are ready to undergo this extension of experience we shall find ourselves enjoying a great deal of *popular art*, instead of fighting against *mass culture*. There are enemies more worthy of attention.

A Note on Folk-song

A word or two on folk-song would be appropriate at this point, for, during the last decade or so, there have been signs of cultural divisions on this front.

To many people, 'folk-singing' is a term that tends to evoke images of a rural and tranquil past, of dancing on the village green, of sunshine and of idyllic love. If the songs are to do with labour, then it is meaningful labour, work that has sense and purpose – like ploughing and sowing, or making a wheel. If the words and tune reflect hardship and sorrow, struggle, grief or pain, then these elements of human existence are seen as desirable abstractions, moulding the life and character of the sufferer and enriching the emotions of the listener. There is a temptation to accept as true folk-songs only those pieces that can be seen through a haze of historical or regional filtering. We are tolerant of sentimentality, eroticism or brutality when it appears in a Northumbrian or Scottish dialect, or when the events and feelings belong to another century, but we pay scant attention to C.N.D. protest songs about nuclear war, contemporary bawdy ballads, or anything in a transatlantic idiom. We struggle to listen to the incoherent, rambling old countryman, but throw up hands in horror at the moaning of Bob Dylan. Some of the reasons for this strange attitude have been hinted at throughout this chapter, and there is also one historical factor to be taken into account.

We have briefly noted, in an earlier chapter, the appearance of 'skiffle' in the 1950's, which lasted but a little while as a separate movement. The emphasis was on home-made music (and instruments to some extent). It was in fact a breakthrough of a folk-song impulse into our century, at a time when pop music was beginning to be seen clearly as, all too often, the soulless product of a commercial machine. Although 'skiffle' as such disappeared, the impetus continued, and over the last ten years there has been a growing popular movement around the title 'folk-music'. Singers have taken contemporary situations and urban settings and made songs about factories, a strike at King's Cross goods-yard, and the hanging of Timothy Evans.[14] Instead of the old anxieties of primitive peoples, worrying about the death of the sun at midwinter, or the failure of crops, and the shadow of infertility, we now have the worry of Strontium Ninety, the mushroom cloud, and the sterility caused by radiation. The old fears are still there. Only the images for them have changed.

Along with this development has been continuing research, in the steps of Cecil Sharp, into old country-songs both here and abroad. Indeed, it may even be significant that in recent years many collectors have spent a great deal of time in backward parts of the world, bringing to us songs in other tongues, rather than attempt the exploration and discrimination needed in the understanding of contemporary offerings here at home. *Shepherd's Hey* is one thing: *St. Pancras Day*, it seems, is quite another.[15] The division of folk-song in this sort of way can be explained in several terms, but the long and short of it all is that professional and reasonably wealthy people, however well intentioned, do *not* have real empathy with those whose work is dull and repetitive, and whose minds are not so receptive to ideas and concepts and abstractions. One has the feeling at times that for some sensitive people, a work-song is only acceptable when the sweat has dried out of it; that a protest song is only reasonable if the issues are dead and buried. Yet surely, folk-music is essentially about live situations and strong feelings, and, though it sounds very pretty preserved in annotated bottles, or given symphonic clothing by Vaughan Williams, its natural function is to reflect and shape the vital feelings of a living community.

If one were to try to sketch in the position of folk-song on the model of musical genres, we should end up with little dots all

[14] Some suggestions for material are made at the end of the book.
[15] From *Songs for the Sixties*, Seeger and MacColl.

over the spectrum of our musics, except perhaps in the most exclusive modern compositions, and the intellectual improvisations of the more esoteric jazz musicians. If we can really bring ourselves to understand both historic *and* contemporary folksong we should find that some goes under its own name, but that a good deal more is called 'Jazz' or 'Pop', and that it has the power to fertilise the music of our contemporary composers. As Sharp himself has said: 'The unconscious output of the human mind, whatever else it may be, is always real and sincere.' It is our task to decide in each particular case whether or not the specific and individual song is an unconscious creation, or just another item from a self-conscious machine.

This is not easy, and we must not confuse 'unconscious output' with anonymity. If we had the appropriate historical tools we would, sooner or later, discover a 'composer' behind many traditional and folk-tunes, and possibly an 'arranger' too. These songs did not grow in fields like cabbages but were shaped by men and women. The individual countryman singing in the local inn is quite conscious, in a sense, of what he is doing. He manages to be aware of the emotions and issues involved and of what his listeners understand and want to hear, and yet, unconsciously, he is able to symbolise these factors into musical experience.

It is tempting to speculate on the similarities between such a singer and composer like Irving Berlin, who, in his enormous output of over a thousand songs, reflects so clearly the particular decade or year. Songs like *Alexander's Rag Time Band* and *White Christmas* certainly catch and to some degree inform the spirit of America at particular times. Berlin, like the folk-singer, could hardly be described as musically literate and he relies heavily on the aural traditions and conventions and an unconscious knack with tunes.

Just how 'real and sincere' is such music? At this point we must face squarely the responsibility of discrimination. Any form of music demands a degree of awareness and control over the materials but derives its quality from the truthfulness of its assumptions about the nature of human feelings. The mere label 'folk-song', or 'pop-song', is not an adequate criterion on which to base judgements of this sort. In fact, we very soon reach the stage when labels become a nuisance because they predispose us to listen in limited ways or not at all.

CHAPTER 6

POPULAR MUSIC IN THE CLASSROOM

"Out of school, adolescents are enthusiastically engaged in musical self-education. They crowd the record shops at week-ends. Within the range of their preferences, they are often knowledgeable and highly critical of performances. They find rhythm exciting. Some teach themselves or each other to play an instrument. Here is a vigorous popular culture which is international in its camaraderie. Yet in the schools, the contrasts are striking."[1]   THE NEWSOM REPORT

WE HAVE seen that popular music is not, in strictly musical terms, a new phenomenon, a product peculiar to this century and our young people. The 'high' and the 'low', the relatively formal and expressive musics have always, in some way or other, coexisted. The most obvious examples of the latter in the twentieth century have been the many styles of jazz, and popular music which is often, though not always, derived from jazz. The relationship between the music of the formal and expressive poles has reached the state of becoming a 'problem' because of the decline of aristocratic and exclusive patrons and the rise of a democracy, because of the efficiency and power of communications and the mass-media, and because of the re-action on the part of some artists, composers and performers of retreat into obscure and esoteric utterance. Those who ought to have been in communication with society at large have not been able to accept this responsibility, and, to fill this gap, a huge commercial machine has taken over.

[1] *Half Our Future*, H.M.S.O.

Added to all this is the fact that adolescents today have much more spending-power and at the same time more uncertainty as to their future. This uncertainty is not simply the result of the threat of nuclear war, though this may play a part, but is rather the product of more years spent undergoing formal education, with the result that marriage and work, those two great stabilisers, are withheld for longer than ever before. The result of this is the production of an adolescent community as distinct from the rest of society, a sub-culture, self-aware and conscious of its differences with the adult world and of its own identity. Like all social groups, this one has a function to make its members feel secure, and because of this, the group is unified around a central banner. Pop music has for some time now functioned in this way, as a signal, a flag, a creed. We must remember, though, that although a particular piece or performer may be used in this way, it is still possible to find real musical value, if we are not deterred from looking by our own set of social signals. The most hopeful sign recently has been the acceptance of certain performers (the Beatles in particular) who have offered something of real musical worth. If we can, in some way or other, draw attention from that which pop music *signalises* to that which is structured, in a *symbolic* form, within the music itself, then we should find common ground between the divisions of our communities. We remember the man pointing his finger.[2] His dog sniffs his hand but his friend looks into the distance. Any sort of music can be used in either of these ways, and, as teachers, we should have an eye towards the horizon.

The Symptoms

Children know as well as anyone else that the most powerful elements in pop music are not really musical ones at all.

'If the main population of people like it then all the others,

[2] Cf. Introduction.

even if they don't like it, like to be with it. So a pop song of today is not really enjoyed so much as digged.'

'I think the girls scream because everyone else screams.'

'As many people say on *Juke Box Jury*, this record is commercial and this is quite important.'

'The Rolling Stones started out being different from everyone else, but they got better.'

'Put these names on your records and they will be a hit.'

'It has a well established performer singing it.'

'It is even better because the Stones wrote it.'

'The Stones are a great group.'

'The Bachelors are the only group that can really sing.'

In the face of attitudes like this, held and expressed in many cases quite uncritically, teachers of music feel at times lost in a world without standards. 'It is easy', say teachers, 'to tell us to use pop music in our lessons, but where does it all lead to? What progress can be made with it?' It is indeed a very knotty problem, for pop music is so emotionally charged and seems to work against the development of children in other 'subjects'. During the first year or so in a secondary school, children seem able and willing, generally speaking, to accept most musical offerings put before them. To fall back on to a simpler, apparently cruder music at around the age of 13 or 14 seems like a regression. For a teacher working in an academic atmosphere, 'progress' is the key-word. He can see young students of mathematics, languages and the sciences making continuous headway, dealing with more and more facts and complex skills. Small wonder, then, that the teacher who has helped his first-year classes to follow the score of a movement of Mozart, or to enjoy some descriptive pieces by Mendelssohn, should feel that pop music in the third year is a negation of progress. But music is not like that. There may be greater complexity, increased subtlety in a Bach fugue compared with, say, *David of the White Rock*, but can we really say that the one is 'better' than the other? Either a work of art is telling the truth or it is not. If its account of the dynamics of human feeling is false or inadequate, we call it 'bad'; if it is true we call it 'good'; and if its truths are profound we call it 'great'. It does not matter whether the feelings are rough or refined, complex in relationships or fairly simple, as long as the musician shapes his conception of sensations without fear of being thought either 'unoriginal' or 'difficult'. We must accept the fact that a child who really understands the significance of a good popular song may well be nearer to real musical understanding than the person who imagines 'pictures' or a 'story' to the music of Beethoven. In this sense at least, there is no such thing as 'progress' in any art.

With this in mind we need not be too discouraged by the changes in attitude between the junior school and adolescence. That such changes do take place is indisputable, and teachers who do not find this are either insensitive, human steamrollers, or just very fortunate. In a very large grammar school, the writer found that in the third year only 11 per cent of the pupils gave classical music as their first preference, compared with 37 per cent in the first year. And yet this need not be an unhealthy sign. It may well be that the musical diet offered in school is not varied enough, or even properly nourishing. A reaction against this might be the best thing.

There is no doubt that in many cases, not enough is made of the very wide musical interests of the younger pupils *before* pop music really becomes anything like a problem. The writer had over 100 12-year-olds list their three favourite pieces, along with performer and composer if known, and in order of preference. Here are a few examples:

1. Mendelssohn's Violin Concerto (Campoli)
2. *Where did our love go?* (Supremes)

3. *If I Fell* (Beatles)

1. *Mars,* from *The Planets* (Holst)
2. Fireworks music (Handel)
3. *Waltzing Matilda* (sung by Frank Ifield)

1. The Duke of Plaza Toro's song, *The Gondoliers* (Sullivan)
2. *A Hard Day's Night* (Beatles)
3. *Pictures at an Exhibition* (Moussorgsky)

1. *Blowing In The Wind* (Marianne Faithful)
2. *Toy Symphony* (Leopold Mozart)
3. Last movement Ninth Symphony (Beethoven)

1. *Peer Gynt Suite* (Grieg)
2. *Where did our love go?* (Supremes)
3. *Eine Kleine Nachtmusik* (Mozart, played by the Boyd Neal Orchestra).

In each case these details were supplied without reference to records or books, entirely unprepared. As it happened, none of these pieces had been heard by those pupils in that particular school, and there is no doubt that, apart from the previous junior school from which they came, these performances were either heard at home on the wireless or the gramophone. In another kind of school, in a different sort of area, such lists may have been less representative of the various genres of music, but they would still be tolerant of a wide range. Two years later, the same pupils seem unable to give such catholic choices, and it may not, in every case, be entirely their fault.

At this earlier age, not only are the actual preferences interesting, but so also are the comments about music.

'Its beat is terrific. I like it when he sings "merci", and when he rolls his tongue.'

'It is the slow, pounding R. and B. beat[3] that gives it that touch of "push" that makes it great.'

[3] Rhythm and Blues.

'Their harmonies and rhythms are so modern and are always pleasing to the ear.'

There were the usual clichés about 'beat' and 'backing' and 'star performers', but in general, the younger pupils give a much more varied account of the music itself than the adolescent groups. There was, for example, this comment on Ravel's *Bolero*.

'This I like because of the way it builds up, first the drums, then the flute and so on. Also the rhythm, and the lively tune. And the way that, towards the end, it becomes powerful and demanding.'

The same boy wrote of *Atlantis* by the Shadows:

'The guitars are blended cleverly, and the string backing adds tone and colour.'

'I like *The House of the Rising Sun* because it is sung with wonderful feeling and expression.'

'*The Rise and Fall of Flingel Bunt* is a fabulous record and I like it because it is weird and played in a wonderful rhythmic way.'

'The second song is a kind of noisy sound and I could listen to it for ever. There is a ringing sound in it which I seem to wait for.'

Would that our potted descriptions of classical pieces were always as full of insight as some of these.

The outstanding impression after hearing the comments of these younger children is the single standard, a musical standard, by which they judge the pieces. Beethoven's 'Ninth' was liked for the 'tune' and for the 'choir singing', which is very similar to comments on the performances of pop groups. The introspections of the lower school seem far less stereotyped than those of the middle school age-group, and we, as teachers, do our share in the petrifying process between these stages.

Standard works on class-teaching of music tend to demonstrate this fact. One such text gives out the usual names of Mozart, Beethoven and Brahms, etc., under the general heading of 'appreciation', and goes on to include Coates, German, Grainger, Grieg, Leodorf and Weinberger. Yet there is no mention of jazz, or indeed any American music at all. Another publication recommends that the programmes of concerts given to schools by professional players should include Weinberger, Grainger, Luigini, German and Coates. There is no mention of either jazz, or even of fairly contemporary composers, including Stravinsky, let alone Schönberg. Many syllabi seem to have the same kind of bias towards light-weight pieces of the last eighty years or so. If a teacher sees fit to spend all his time on the great 'masters', fair enough; but so much of the material that is used is really second rate, and museum second rate at that. It is not only a poor specimen of a beast, but dead and stuffed as well.

There are, of course, exceptional books and exceptional teachers, but there are also others who really need to rediscover living music once again. Two publications in particular are giving something of a lead as far as musical material is concerned. One of them[4] offers all kinds of songs, with wide cultural implications, as well as the more usual pieces. The other[5] includes in its list of suggested material, songs by Copland, Hindemith, Williamson, Seiber, Benjamin and Finzi and many contemporary English writers. If this reflects a general tendency then things are more promising than they were.

Whatever the position may be, we have one clear line of attack on the problem of the 'middle-school'. We must make an attempt to remove some of the more useless prejudices that surround pop music, by concentrating attention on the music itself. We do not fight it, ignore it, or just put up with it,

---

[4] *Something to Sing*, Geoffrey Brace.
[5] *Handbook for Music Teachers*, Ed. Rainbow (vol. 2). There are of course, other useful books and collections, and some are noted at the end of the book.

instead we try to discover the essence of particular pieces and work from there.

Preparation

The first and most important factor is the attitude of the teacher. Pop music is emotionally charged 'and therefore treacherous territory for the teacher, and certainly studies in this area should only be conducted by teachers who themselves can respond to popular music and recognise that it has a validity of its own'.[6] The first stage must therefore be 'preparation' in the rigorous sense; listening to music of this sort without distraction, and if possible, with the help of a discriminating enthusiast. It is the personal experience of the writer that at times the enthusiasm of a schoolboy has led to the discovery of hitherto unknown musical possibilities, not only as regards popular music, but in other, more complex areas too. It is more difficult to prepare in this way than one might think at first, for we overhear so much pop music in odd snatches from time to time and this is, of course, not at all the same thing as listening. The danger is that we may deceive ourselves into believing otherwise. We must listen as we should to, say, a recording of a string quartet, more than once, and with an open mind as far as possible. An evening spent with Radio One is an easy way to begin. If anything turns up that seems to ring true it may well be worth investing in a 'single' record. But listening is the key-word: it is not enough to have the sound going on whilst marking G.C.E. harmony papers.

The second stage should be to try to build popular music into the syllabus. To use pop as 'light relief' at the end of term is a fairly common habit and a poor one, for it inclines once more towards the cultural divisions: it admits that the teacher feels the pressures that adolescents can apply via popular music, and yet indicates that the teacher will not consider it

[6] *The Popular Arts*, op. cit.

seriously *as* music. If it is to be used at all it must be not as a 'let out', but as a *way in*. The teacher will, in the regular employment of popular numbers, avoid whenever possible the really insubstantial and diluted pieces, just as he should avoid any 'light' classical pieces with similar disabilities. Any attempt to engage the full attention and sympathy of adolescents will fail if the musical material is not completely sincere and meaningful, whatever the style. Teenagers, like anyone else, can overlook the weaknesses of music played as they dance or talk in the coffee bar, but in the classroom only the best is good enough.

The question arises as to how popular songs should be approached in analysis. We might ask this question of any music, but it is important not to push detailed probing too far with pop, since expressive music is easily 'killed' in this way, and it might look, to the pupils, like deliberate murder. We might consider as models two Beatles songs from the past, originally issued in 1965 on one single record.

Ticket to Ride is basically a fairly bright number, derived in feeling from Negro 'railroad' blues. It is worth noticing a number of details. The use of various percussive noises is quite subtle, and provides a stimulation of musical responses in the listener, rather than provokes the hypnotic reaction of, say, *Money*. The regular syncopation at the phrase ends is a good example of this device used consistently, and could be removed from context to show both the effect and the notation (Example 17). This could make a teaching point and might be followed up by attempts to improvise or compose a simple tune, but with syncopation of this sort.

Example 17

I think I'm gonna be sad——— I think It's to-day ——— Yeh —

——— The girl that's driving me mad— Is go-ing a way——— etc.

An interesting effect is achieved by the use of the same melodic event at the words 'I think its today', and 'is going away'. A class able to understand that the refreshing change of harmony the second time *seems* to alter the tune, will have gained in musical experience. In the same kind of way, the slight alterations at the end of the phrases on the repeated title-lines provide a neat example of a simple variant in each case. If all three lines were the same it would be boring, but the second time has the well-known Beatles melisma – 'She's got a ticket to ri – hi – hide', and the third version has the flat blues seventh, which in performance strains upwards, making almost a major interval before the resolution, which, by the way, produces a three-bar phrase (Example 18).

Example 18

We might notice also the 'train-whistle' intervals of 'driving me mad', and the extremely high notes in the coda-fade out (top 'D' in performance) giving what sounds almost like an imitation of the 'baby' who doesn't care. The whole song is contained within a framework of rhythm, harmony and instrumental timbre, and the result is something more than just a burp of personal feeling, or mild hypnosis. The total effect is, in fact, pleasing; we have the feeling of pleasure that comes from experiencing something well done.

Yes It Is, on the other side of the original recording,[7] is quite different. It is a slow, blues-derived song, notated accurately in

[7] Parlophone R 35265, but also on other issues.

triplet rhythm. The blues beat is restrained and, in the best tradition, does not get any faster from beginning to end. This implies a degree of *control*, not always present in pop songs. The textural background is also well under control, and at times quite delicate. The verse is pentatonic, and the harmonica, with its octave leaps at the end of phrases, provides a kind of framework, or edging, within which the song is shaped. We may notice the odd bar with only two beats which forces the second verse into action more promptly than usual. This seems to reflect the slight feeling of anxiety to tell the story, to make the point that red clothes will bring back memories. Both the duplets and the *tenuto* style of singing of 'Yes – it – is', and the extension in the second verse to 'Yes it is its true, Yes it is', add to the impression of a mechanical excuse rather than a broken-hearted statement of lost love. 'Scarlet were the clothes she wore' seems in this context a deliberate dramatisation of the past in archaic terms; a display of faithfulness in the face of a possible new relationship with the unknown person to whom the song is addressed. The climax is most effective; a piling up of sound to make an affirmation, and then again, the suspicion, with the whispered 'Yeh', that the singer is trying to convince himself (Example 19).

Example 19

If I could forget her But it's my pride yes it is yes it is   Oh yes it is   is Yeh – – – –   *etc.*

The whole feeling of the song is unsettled, the motives are not clear, the hinted relationship with the mysterious listener is as unresolved as the harmonies in the vocal parts. Even the little harmonica decoration at the very end seems to put the question. 'If you wear red?' The insistence on a previous relationship in the face of a new one is the most fascinating feature which both words and music convey unerringly. Whether the whole thing is a fluke, or a conscious or unconscious creation, does not matter: the song is worth hearing more than once, it has something to say to any age group. But notice particularly the analogy between the emotional and social state of the adolescent and the feeling of this piece. There seems to be in this, and in other pop songs, a reflection of the interaction of the two worlds of the adolescent: the dichotomy between the old world of childhood, no longer adequate, but secure and known, and the new realm of the adult, unknown, rather frightening, but an essential and needed development. It is a song of relationships, and it presents real issues in a symbolic way. To understand it is to know more of the motion, interplay, and development of human feelings.

Practical Possibilities

It is difficult, though not impossible. to get to grips with the *meaning* of any music in a classroom. Popular music is by no means an exception to this. If it can happen it is extremely worthwhile. We might call this particular approach 'straightforward analysis', and, generally speaking, it is better to start in some other way until good relationships with the pupils make it possible. Another alternative, more difficult than it sounds, is performance, that is to say, the singing of pop songs as part of the repertory. The teacher must be quite sure that he can make the piano sound like a reasonable imitation of the guitar, or whatever accompaniment on the recording. This is not easy. The copy is often no guide at all, and the chords and progressions will not fit naturally under the fingers of one used to Bach, Chopin, Beethoven and hymn-tunes. Neither will the rhythm flow well unless the player is able to relax into the style. An alternative is to sing with the record. There are also problems of copyright and the price of songs.[8] Generally speaking, the words on the board and the tune by rote will be the

[8] Northern Songs publish collections of Beatles songs, words only, tunes and words with guitar, or piano and vocal line.

rule. There are other lines of approach which are not quite so hazardous.

Direct comparison with other pieces of music can be useful in clearing the air. A science master in an Essex school[9] ran a course on mass-media and used pop music to a large extent. 'The method was to ask children to bring their disks. Four of these (or parts of them) were used each lesson. I found four pieces of music which 'matched' the pop music in some way – in theme, in style, in instruments, in volume – anything.' A system of scoring was agreed upon by the children, on things like rhythm, melody and clear words and good arrangement. A good deal of discussion was caused by the results when classical pieces and pop songs were scored in this kind of way. The pop scores seemed relatively too low. It was found that, to make the scores seem 'right', they should have included such things as 'Is the singer good-looking?' or 'Is he on TV?' or 'Is this in the top ten?' and so on, thus recognising that their main interests were *not* musical ones. Group solidarity and status and erotic sensation were the real criteria. Mr. Leech points out that the lessons were in no way 'destructive or cynical in character', and he also gives a hint about the cultural pressures from some of his colleagues. 'Pressure was put upon me to refer to all their selections as "tripe", "rubbish" and "nonsense" as a form of indoctrination. This would have been fatal.'

Comparison and an Experiment

Some time before Mr. Leech had given this description of his approach, the writer had completed a third experiment in his own school.[10] The aim this time was to measure the attitude of pupils to a test-piece of classical music, after a sustained and deliberate attempt had been made to eliminate some of the negative cultural factors. Once again a score was taken on a

[9] Mr. D. Leech.
[10] Cf. Chapter 4.

ten-point scale to establish a kind of norm from which to calculate change of attitudes. Four academically streamed groups of third-year boys were divided into two main sections, A and C being the experimental section and B and D the control. Over a period of four weeks the control groups B/D were taught along the lines of the established music syllabus in the school. The topic was 'Russian Composers', and included were pieces like the *Polovstian Dances* (Borodin), *Night on a Bare Mountain* (Moussorgsky) and the Finale of Tchaikovsky's Fourth Symphony. In the middle of a period in the fifth week, the test-piece (once again a Haydn last movement) was played. Scoring took place as before, the appropriate term being ticked off on the questionnaire.

The experimental groups, A/C, on the other hand, were not taught from any preformed syllabus of this kind. The objective was to juxtapose wherever possible, music from classical and popular sources. In each case an attempt was made to find common musical grounds for comparison and criticism, and to by-pass the implications of 'our' music and 'school' music. When no strong artistic link could be found then attention was directed to anything at all that the musics had in common. An account was kept of what transpired. It was, of course, a strange assortment, since the boys brought their own records, often without prior notice of what they were. The teacher's role was to find something in the cupboard that offered comparison and opportunity for discussion. (It is, of course, much better to know what is coming beforehand to make preparation possible.) Topics were eventually suggested from week to week, such as 'music from films', and 'music' with a lively rhythm, anything in fact to enable the aim of alignment to be fulfilled. Here are some examples of lessons of this sort.

    Topic – *Music for films*
        (a) *The Frightened City* (Shadows)
        (b) *Peace Pipe* (Shadows)

    (c) Part of *Sinfonia Antarctica* (Vaughan Williams)

    (d) Prelude to *Ben Hur* (Rozsa)

    (e) *Walking* (Shadows)

    (f) The 'storm' from the *Pastoral Symphony* (Beethoven).

Two of the points for discussion were: Is the music effective and helpful to the scene or action? Can it be enjoyed *without* the picture? In this particular case it was felt that (a), (c) and (f) were particularly effective in the film context. (The Beethoven movement was not given a name to begin with, but described merely as 'from Walt Disney's *Fantasia*'.) The class seemed to agree that the *Ben Hur* piece was the least effective without the film, which shows well-developed powers of discrimination. An interesting comment came from one jazz/pop fan. 'Sir, when you said Walt Disney, I wanted to like the music because I like Walt Disney, and I *did* like it; but if you had said 'Beethoven', I would not have wanted to listen.' This is a very clear statement of the position. A willingness to listen is half the battle, and it is just this willingness that pop inhibits *if* we allow the cultural elements to get in the way. Let us take another example.

Topic – *Instrumental sounds*

    (a) *Wonderful Land* (Shadows)

    (b) *Nutrocker* ('B. Bumble')

    (c) March from *Nutcracker Suite* (Tchaikovsky)

    (d) *Marche Royale* from *The Soldier's Tale* (Stravinsky)

    (e) *Stranger on the Shore* (Acker Bilk)

    (f) *Rondo* from Clarinet Concerto (Mozart).

Many thought that (a) would become 'boring' if played often; (b) was found exciting and (d) interesting; (e) and (f) were played twice in part, because discussion broke out on the different styles of clarinet playing.

  'Acker Bilk puts his own expression into it; the tune on its own is not much good.'

'Mozart used higher notes; his piece is more difficult to play and more complicated to listen to.'

It is pretty obvious who were at the top of the charts at this time, but the same kind of thing works just as well with different names. Not all of the pieces used were good of their kind, and the striking thing is that this was pointed out by the pupils.

In the middle of the fifth session of this sort the Haydn test-piece was once again played and was scored as before. The results of this test, compared with the results of the control groups B/D, are significant. Neither academic ability nor previously stated preferences for various types of music seemed to hold back the experimental groups. On average, groups A/C *gained* over half a point on the ten-point scale, while the control groups, B/D, *lost* over half a point. The greatest gains with A/C were with those who did not include classical music as a preference in the first place.[11] The striking difference between these results and the results of previously conducted experiments with different groups of children, is that the scores are conditioned by the kind of lessons and the sort of musical material that each group had dealings with. In the first place, the test-piece was played without explanation or relation to the popular music that preceded it, with the effect that the two sorts of music were seen in stark contrast with all their opposing cultural aura. With the experimental groups in the last test, time was taken to establish objective listening, not just to allow a projection of subjective feelings onto the music. This is what we mean by 'comparison'. It is a way into the situation and whatever other approaches may be used, an element of

[11] These experiments are here and in Chapter 4 described with the minimum amount of detail. The reader will have to take on trust the fact that the whole project was controlled in a strict manner; that different groups of pupils were used and different experimenters; and that the results were broken down in great detail. The results were in every case significant, and simply confirm all that has been said about the cultural, as opposed to the musical significance, of popular music, and the attitudes of pupil and teacher.

comparing across the various musical cultures is bound, sooner or later, to be present.

Old Popular Music, Jazz, and the 'Low' Music of Other Centuries

'Old pops' are useful in the classroom. Because they have once been popular they command attention, and yet are fairly free for teacher and pupil of external associations. We have to be careful not to use pieces that have recently been ousted by the current favourites, for the simple reason that there may well be an element of friction within the class because of this. Not every pupil climbs on to the bandwagon: some of them change more slowly and with a certain amount of reluctance to new idols. However, older pieces can be helpful. During the final experiment described above, some of the boys said that a year or so back they had found *Wonderful Land* exciting and had all bought a recording. But, they said, they heard it so many times that it become 'boring'. By bringing it to school after a longish period of time they were able to find it attractive once more, and probably this second wave of appreciation was much more acute, because the effects of high-pressure salesmanship and adolescent culture had diminished. Teacher and pupils were listening to the same music in the same kind of way. A year before, they would have been on opposite sides of the fence, not really hearing the thing at all. By using the older pieces from time to time some idea of its ephemeral nature can be imparted. 'Here today and gone tomorrow' just about sums it up and yet, some of yesterday's offerings are worth preserving. This is a step towards recognising that even music hundreds of years old may be worth attention.

It is but one step from older popular pieces into jazz. Children, as we have said before, are not usually very fond of jazz in general, though sometimes particular pieces are adopted by the pop world. Occasionally people like Brubeck and Armstrong get into the 'charts'. If this happens, we can use the piece as a lever to open up the frontiers of jazz. It is not really so very far from Armstrong's version of *Hello Dolly*, to his *Potato Head Blues*, a really fine example of jazz in 1927. If children and teacher become tolerant of jazz they will find in it many musical excitements and a tremendous range of styles. *Dr. Jazz* has already been mentioned,[12] and the classic recording by Jelly Roll Morton is worth hearing many times. Morton was one of the great individualists but also able to assimilate many influences. His piano style in *The Crave* is more than just reminiscent of the Spanish *habanera*, and would compare well with Debussy's *La Puerta del Vino*, or the famous song from Bizet's *Carmen*. Likewise, the trumpet playing of Armstrong in *Potato Head* could be compared with players like Kenny Ball or classical players playing Vivaldi, or the Haydn concerto, or again with the careful and delicate playing of Miles Davis in say, *Milestones*. As part of a study of possibilities in sound with bigger bands we could look at Ellington's *Hot and Bothered*, or some of the scores of Dankworth, or at something by Count Basie. We might compare the sounds of smaller groups, like Brubeck's *Take Five* or *Django* by the Modern Jazz Quartet, with the March from Schönberg's *Serenade*, or with the Royal March from Stravinsky's *The Soldier's Tale*. We could look for the traces of jazz in classical composers: Copland's *Dance Symphony*, or his *Four Piano Blues*, or Lambert's *The Rio Grande*. Once the doors of jazz are opened there is no limit to the variety and to the possibilities of comparison with classical pieces.

Old popular songs and jazz can both lead beyond themselves, back into music history; to older folk-songs and ballads, to the music-hall and to the incantations of primitive peoples.[13] Anyone can see the similarity between the music of remote Asian and African communities and with the earliest country blues of

[12] Unfortunately, at this present time there is not one record company able to supply *Dr. Jazz*. It will certainly be released again sooner or later.

[13] A useful sourcebook would be *Popular Music of the Olden Time* by William Chappell.

America. Weill's *The Threepenny Opera* could take us back to John Gay and *The Beggar's Opera*, and from that point it is not difficult to introduce something of Handel's work, even if it is only to show why Gay wanted to simplify the music and liven up the plot. In one way or another, we can start with the 'low' music of our century and go back in time, and once we have taken the pupils with us it is fairly easy to show the 'high' music of the same period. ('Low' and 'high' have been useful words for us, but perhaps for classroom use we should choose others.) Needless to say, it is left to the teacher to find the best way of presentation for him and the class.

Some Specific Projects

'Songs of protest' makes a good focus for lots of music, and reflects the mood of teenagers. Why not look at some C.N.D. songs? Safer ground might be to trace back songs with political implications or social messages in a more general way. Donovan with *The Universal Soldier*, and Woody Guthrie, and blues and spirituals are full of social comment, and could be linked up with the teaching of social history. The *Colour Bar Strike*,[14] by a fireman at King's Cross, is worth some attention, and there are the possibilities of arranging different accompaniments for all the eight verses, or of handing round the characters to various pupils, or of dramatising it in the form of a union meeting. It is well worth the trouble to find a recording of Pete Seeger singing in Carnegie Hall,[15] *Who Killed Davy Moore?*, and explore its implications for boxing enthusiasts. It is also a song worth singing. A comparison of this kind of song with *Men of Harlech* or *We Be Three Poor Mariners*, or with *The Beggar*, promises interesting results beyond the actual subject matter of the words. The idea that we can enjoy singing con-

---

[14] *The Singing Island*, compiled by Peggy Seeger and Ewan MacColl, Mills Music.

[15] On an L.P. CBS 62209 BPG (*We Shall Overcome*, No. 3).

tradictory sentiments if the tune is good, is enlightening, and makes for tolerance and understanding of other points of view, as well as extending the range of feeling and emotion, in a symbolic and therapeutic way.

A study of mass-media is always valuable and can be extended to books, films and TV. It is often enlightening to get pupils to build up a diagram to show the evolution of a pop song. It might look something like the diagram on this page.

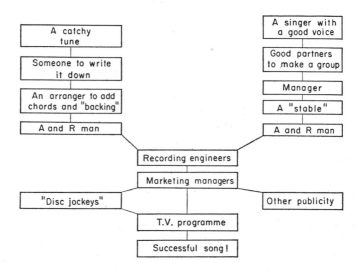

This could be contrasted with the simpler forms of transmission, where the performers and singers are the same person. Sooner or later the pupils will realise the dangers of such a complex journey for such small and simple songs. At nearly every stage someone is going to interfere with the song: the manager, the A and R man, the recording engineers, the arrangers and the hired orchestra or extra voices brought in to form a background choir, will take away in most cases any freshness and vitality that the piece may have had at the start.

Some manage to survive. There is also the additional danger that some songs will be aimed at the widest possible public, including mum and dad. For this reason a lively and sincere performer will sometimes be covered over with wailing strings and heavenly choirs to appease the ears and win the affections of older people. *Take These Chains From My Heart* is a case in point, and yet Ray Charles, the singer, is well able to give a fine account of really expressive songs in the blues style. This is unfortunately liable to happen in any attempt to superimpose the devices and sounds of classical music onto the basic line of jazz-derived popular songs.

The Beatles are still the best performers of their own songs, and arrangements for orchestra by George Martin, or renderings by the Hollyridge Orchestra, merely sprinkle sugar on to spices. The attempt by one of our singers of opera to sing pop songs in the style of Mozart is a similar miscalculation. We certainly want to cross and recross the divisions of our music, but we must never mix them all together into a tasteless stew. Each piece should be distinctive. We want to widen the musical palate, not paralyse the buds of taste. The same danger exists, though not so acutely, in the attempt to underpin the transient music of jazz and the ephemeral brevity of pop with classical forms and devices. Brubeck has attempted this in his *Rondo a la Turk*. The Swingles have taken baroque music and simply changed the sound without making any formal alteration. This can be a good point of comparison – the Swingles and the Stuttgart Chamber Orchestra playing the same piece. In fact, the Swingles come out of it rather well and whatever else we might say, their performance is certainly musical. (One thinks particularly of the slow movement of a Handel harpsichord concerto.)

A project on 'dancing' might be a good approach with girls. There is endless scope here, not only to listen to the music but perhaps to learn the steps as well. In this way they would learn what enjoyment there might be in a whole range of dances, including, rock 'n roll, the tango, the polka, the waltz, the minuet and country dances. The music for each of these would be absorbed perhaps without much comment, but it would give a first-rate experience of all kinds of music from Playford to Parnell.

The study of one work from a composer who cuts across our cultural barriers would also be very useful as a starting-point. Bernstein's *West Side Story* springs to mind, or perhaps something from Gershwin. A comparison between *West Side Story* and Tchaikovsky's *Romeo and Juliet* overture seems almost too obvious to mention. Copland has a concerto for clarinet and orchestra which has a beautiful cadenza between its two main movements where the clarinet initiates a 'swing' out of which the last section evolves. The development from classical to jazz in this way is extremely effective and very convincing.[16]

The simplest, and perhaps most honest approach to begin with, might be called 'Music I Don't Understand'. This might include *musique concréte*, the music of Cage or Boulez or Berio, Indian music, some modern jazz and some surrealist pop music. There are plenty of Beatles examples of the latter, including some of the *Sgt. Pepper* numbers.[17] On the frontiers of musical experience we are all equal. The teacher and the kids can enlighten each other. The great thing is to get started.

Conclusion

In some rural communities and in schools where there is a lot of really active music-making, and not so much talking and listening, it may well transpire that the problem of pop never rears its head. If so, we should be grateful for the respite, but also a little uneasy about being out of touch with some elements of contemporary experience. Whatever we may like to think, this is not the most common state of affairs at the

[16] There is a recording by Benny Goodman.
[17] *Sergeant Pepper's Lonely Hearts Club Band*, Parlophone: PMC 7027.

moment. The more usual picture is of a music teacher struggling to make his music heard, sometimes literally, over the froth and bubble of an ever-present popular culture. Let us be honest. By bringing popular music and its relations into the classroom we shall not, *ipso facto*, have solved all our problems of class control and attention. That is so much a matter of personality and organisation. What we shall have done is to break a rather vicious circle of prejudice and ignorance between the age and social groups in which we find ourselves. We cannot go back to the days of rural values and rural folk-song, and the alternative is to be discerning about the present, testing the ground as we explore and trying to find any clues we can to help us discriminate between the better and the weaker offerings. In this way our ears will at least be open to the music of the people, the folk-music of our time.

It is not impossible to see the most lively of all the arts spanning, as it appeared to do in the 'Golden Age', the whole range of our society. Until there are composers and performers who can be clearly seen and accepted as a centre of reconciliation, it is the responsibility of the teacher, the educator, to refrain from driving the thin edge of the wedge into the musical development of the young. Our advertisers and business-men manage only too often to perform this function. It is up to the educationalist to lead away from sterile attitudes and specious generalisations, back into the quality of the particular and the specific, back into music itself, no matter what name it has been given. For who knows, we could be shaping a new and undivided community.

BIBLIOGRAPHY
and List of Material

*ALDERSON, C., *Magazines Teenagers Read*, Pergamon, 1967.
BLESH, R., *Shining Trumpets: A History of Jazz*, London: Cassell, 1949.
BRACE, G., *Something to Sing*, O.U.P.
BRAUN, M., *Love Me Do: The Beatles' Progress*, Penguin, 1964.
BROWN, J. A. C., *Techniques of Persuasion*, Penguin, 1963.
CASSIRER, E., *An Essay on Man: An Introduction to a Philosophy of Human Culture*, New Haven: Yale University Press, 1944.
CHAPPEL, W., *Popular Music of the Olden Time*, New York: Dover, 1915.
COOKE, D., *The Language of Music*, O.U.P., 1959.
DUNWELL, W., *Music and the European Mind*, London: Jenkins, 1962.
FARNSWORTH, P. R., *The Social Psychology of Music*, New York: Dryden Press, 1958.
*FLEMING, C. M., *Adolescence: Its Social Psychology*, London: Routledge, revised 2nd edition, 1963.
GOMBRICH, E. H., *Art and Illusion: A Study in the Psychology of Pictorial Representation*, London: Phaidon Press, 1960.
*HALL, S. and WHANNEL, P., *The Popular Arts*, London: Hutchinson, 1964.
Handbook for Music Teachers, Ed. BERNARR RAINBOW. London: Novello, 1964.
HARRIS, R., *Jazz*, Pelican, 1952.
HECHINGER, G. and F. M., *Teenage Tyranny*, London: Duckworth, 1964.
HOGGART, R., *The Uses of Literacy*, Penguin, 1958.
KOESTLER, A., *Insight and Outlook*, London: Macmillan, 1949.
LAMBERT, C., *Music Ho!* Penguin, 1948.
LANG, P. H., *Music in Western Civilisation*, New York: Norton, 1941.
LANGER, S. K., *Feeling and Form*, London: Routledge, 1953.
LANGER, S. K., *Philosophy in a New Key*, O.U.P., 1951.
LEAVIS, F. R. and THOMPSON, D., *Culture and Environment*, Chatto & Windus, 1942.
LIPTON, L., *The Holy Barbarians*, London: Allen, 1960.
MACKERNESS, E. D., *A Social History of English Music*, London: Routledge, 1964.
MAUGHAM, S. W., *Theatre*, London: Heinemann, 1953.
MELLERS, W., *Music and Society*, London: Dobson, 2nd edition, 1946.
*MELLERS, W., *Music in a New Found Land*, London: Barrie & Rockliff, 1964.
MELLERS, W., *Music in the Making*, London: Dobson, 1952.
New Oxford History of Music, Ed. E. WELLESZ, O.U.P., 1957.
NEWSOM REPORT, *Half Our Future*, London: H.M.S.O., 1966.
*NEWTON, F., *The Jazz Scene*, Penguin, 1961.

* Particularly useful.

PLEASANTS, H., *Death of a Music: The Decline of the European Tradition and The Rise of Jazz*, London: Gollancz, 1961.

RICHMOND, K. W., *Culture and General Education*, London: Methuen, 1963.

SACHS, C., *Rhythm and Tempo: A Study in Musical History*, London: Dent, 1953.

*SARGANT, W., *Battle for the Mind*, London: Pan Books, 1957.

SCHOLES, P. A., *The Oxford Companion to Music*, O.U.P., 9th edition, 1955.

SEASHORE, C. E., *Psychology of Music*, New York: McGraw-Hill, 1938.

SILBERMANN, A., *The Sociology of Music*, London: Routledge, 1963.

SPAETH, S., *A History of Popular Music in America*, London: Phoenix, 1960.

THOMPSON, D., *Discrimination and Popular Culture*, Penguin, 1964.

WILLIAMS, R., *Culture and Society*, London: Chatto, 1960.

WILLIAMS, R., *Communications*, Penguin, 1962.

ZACHRY, C. B., *Emotion and Conduct in Adolescence*, New York: Appleton-Century, 1940.

* Particularly useful.

ARTICLES

Observer, various contributions from 1963 to 1964.

Melody Maker, various pieces from 1963 to 1964.

Musical Times, various pieces in 1964.

New Society, an article by H. L. Wilensky, 14th May, 1964.

New Statesman, various contributions from 1963 to 1964.

Punch, an article by Brubeck, May 1964.

SHEET MUSIC

Bits and Pieces, Clark and Smith, pub. Ardmore and Beechwood, 1961.

Doctor Jazz, Melrose and Oliver, pub. Melrose, New York, 1927.

Ev'rybody's Twistin', Kochler and Bloom, pub. Mills Music Co., 1962.

With You In Mind, West and Ornadel, pub. Ardmore and Beechwood, 1961.

The Various Beatles' Songs are published by Northern Songs, 1963–1967.

SONG COLLECTIONS RELEVANT TO CHAPTER 6

Burl Ives' Song Book, Ballantine.

Oxford School Music Books. Particularly Senior Book 3. DOBBS and FISKE, O.U.P.

The Shuttle and the Cage. Industrial Folk-ballads edited by EWAN MACCOLL, Workers' Music Association, 1954.

The Singing Island. A collection of English and Scots folk-songs compiled by PEGGY SEEGER and EWAN MACCOLL, Mills Music, 1960.

Something to Sing. A collection ranging from Mozart to "Casey Jones" compiled by GEOFFREY BRACE, Cambridge University Press, 1963 (Books 1 and 2 in particular).

Songs for the Sixties. A provocative collection of contemporary songs edited by PEGGY SEEGER and EWAN MACCOLL, Workers' Music Association, 1961.

Songs of the New World. A collection of the best-known American traditional songs and ballads, DESMOND MACMAHON, McDougall.

Various Beatles Collections, published by Northern Songs, are worth considering, particularly books of fifty tunes with guitar notation. In addition here are three useful pieces of pop-pastiche suitable for classroom performance.

The Daniel Jazz, HERBERT CHAPPELL, Novello.

Jonah-man Jazz, MICHAEL HURD, Novello (easier than the above).

Notions in the Pop-art idiom for teen-age groups. GEOFFREY RUSSELL-SMITH, Novello, 1965. (A rather dated style now, but some interesting ideas for recorders and has an incorporated canon.)

Note: These lists of material and records are not intended to be comprehensive. They indicate specific material mentioned in the book in the hope that the uninitiated will have a starting-point for their own exploration.

GRAMOPHONE RECORDS

The following is a brief sample from the material indicated in Chapter 6. Where practicable, particular recordings are suggested, but the reader is warned that records are withdrawn and reissued at an alarming rate, and by the time of publication some of these will be out of date. The best course of action for those who are not sure of material is to spend an hour or so in a record shop with a friendly proprietor, who will allow customers to sample various recordings. In this way it is possible to build up a picture of the current scene and, in so doing, extend one's own powers of discrimination. (It is assumed that a list of 'classical' recordings is unnecessary.)

Folk

Lord of the Dance, SYDNEY CARTER (Electra EPK 801).
Notice in particular *Friday Morning* with its implications of Christian belief.

We Shall Overcome—No. 3, PETE SEEGER (CBS BPG62209).
This is a recording from Carnegie Hall in 1963. Two songs that have a strong element of social comment are *Who Killed Norma Jean?* and *Who Killed Davey Moore?*

The Iron Muse A. L. LLOYD and others (Topic Records 12 T 86).
A panorama of industrial folk song.

The Collier's Rant, LOUIS KILLEN and JOHNNY HANDLE (Topic 74).
Mining songs of the Northumbrian and Durham coalfields.

Bob Dylan's Greatest Hits (CBS BPG 62847).
Not everyone would class Dylan as a folk-singer, but notice in particular the qualities of *The Times They Are A-Changin'* and *Mr. Tambourine Man.*

Topic Records have recently issued a wide-ranging series of folk-music recordings. Their catalogue of over 100 titles is available: Topic Records Ltd., 27 Nassington Road, London N.W.3.

Jazz

Krooked Blues, KING OLIVER and the Creole Jazz Band.
> A fine example of traditional jazz at a slow tempo with a great deal of tone and pitch 'bending'.

King Porter Stomp, JELLY ROLL MORTON. A master of jazz piano style.

The Crave, JELLY ROLL MORTON. Strong suggestion of the *habanera*.

Doctor Jazz, MORTON. If a recording is available.

Muskat Ramble, ARMSTRONG. Or any of the 'Hot Five' recordings.

Out Came the Blues, A useful collection (Ace of Hearts 158).

Hot and Bothered, DUKE ELLINGTON. Famous recording of 1927.

King Porter Stomp, BENNY GOODMAN. An example of the 'swing' style of the 1940's. Compare with Morton's version.

Applecake, JOHNNY DANKWORTH (Parl. GEP8653). A superb demonstration of the sound and technique of the big band.

Leapfrog, PARKER and GILLESPIE (Columbia SEB 10087).
> An 'up-tempo' piece showing the technique and extended phrasing of these musicians.

Milestones, MILES DAVIS (Philips TFE 17223). Delicate and sensitive trumpet playing.

Take Five, from BRUBECK's Greatest Hits (CBS 62710). Notice the extended drum improvisation in the L.P. version that was cut from the E.P. release.

One Never Knows, MODERN JAZZ QUARTET. Note the complex counterpoint.

Pop

It is impossible to list current favourites, but over the last few years three groups seem to merit particular attention. (These suggestions are intended merely to help the teacher to find his bearings, if he has not already done so, in the world of pop music. Many teachers will be able to collect material quite easily through children at school.)

MANFRED MANN, *As Is* (Fontana TL 5377).
> Notice the experimental aspects of *You're My Girl*, the 'drive' of *Dealer*, and the near sentimentality of *A Now and Then Thing*.

THE SHADOWS, *Greatest Hits* (Columbia 33SX 1522).
> They manage to combine a pop sound with sensitive and skilful instrumental technique. Notice the atmospheric nature of *The Frightened City*.

THE BEATLES,   *Yes It Is/Ticket To Ride* (Parlophone R5265).
> *With The Beatles* (PMC 1206). Includes *Not A Second Time* and *All I've Got To Do*.
> *A Collection of Beatles Oldies* (PMC 2016).
> Includes *Eleanor Rigby* and *Ticket to Ride, Can't Buy Me Love* and *She Loves You*.
> *Sgt. Pepper* (PMC 7027).

ACKNOWLEDGEMENTS FOR QUOTATIONS

Ardmore & Beechwood Ltd.: *With You In Mind* and *Bits And Pieces*. *Art and Illusion* by E. H. Gombrich. Bollingen Series XLV. 5. The A. W. Mellon Lectures in the Fine Arts. 1956. Copyright 1960 by the Trustees of the National Gallery of Art, Washington, D.C. Published by the Princeton University Press. J. M. Dent & Sons Ltd.: *Music in Western Civilisation*, also W. W. Norton & Co. Dennis Dobson: *Music in the Making*, W. Mellers. Doubleday & Co. and The Literary Executor of W. Somerset Maugham and Heinemann Ltd: *Theatre*. John Farquharson Ltd. and Paul R. Reynolds Inc.: *Death of a Music*, H. Pleasants. H.M.S.O.: *Half Our Future*. Hutchinson and Random House Inc.: *The Popular Arts*, Hall and Whannel. McGraw-Hill Book Co.: *Psychology of Music*, C. E. Seashore. *Melody Maker*. *New Statesman*: article by Paul Johnson, letter by Deryck Cooke. Northern Songs Ltd.: copyright 1963, 1964 and 1965, songs by John Lennon and Paul McCartney. Oxford University Press: *New Oxford History of Music* and *Oxford Companion to Music*. Penguin Books Ltd.: *Jazz*, Rex Harris, and *Techniques of Persuasion*, J. A. C. Brown. Peter Maurice Music Co. Ltd.: *Ev'rybody's Twistin'*. Laurence Pollinger Ltd. and Alfred A. Knopf Inc.: *Shining Trumpets*, Rudi Blesh, also Cassell & Co. Ltd. Dr. William Sargant: *Battle for the Mind*. Routledge & Kegan Paul Ltd.: *Feeling and Form*, S. K. Langer; *A Social History of English Music*, E. D. Mackerness; *The Sociology of Music*, A. Silbermann.

Thanks are also due to Professor G. H. Bantock for his help

in preparing the original thesis; to Mr. D. Leech for his information; to Mrs. J. Kinder for her assistance and encouragement with the experimental work; to Peter Polfreman for his help with the original manuscript; to Mr. J. W. Lugg for all his work in preparing the musical examples; and to my wife for her proof-reading and patience.

INDEX

A and R man   60, 124
Adolescence as a sub-culture   70
Adolescent needs   69–72
Aesthetic basis of music   2–6
ALDERSON, CONNIE, *Magazines Teen-
    agers Read*   78
All in the April Evening   98
Amateur musician   8
American music   18–19
    see also Jazz
ARMSTRONG, LOUIS   25, 59, 96, 121,
    122
Avant-garde composers   96

BACH
    Two Part Invention in E Major
        36
    Three Part Invention in E Minor
        37–38
Bar-line, introduction of   11
Baroque music   11
B.B.C. as patron   21
"Beat" music   94
Beatlemania   85
BEATLES   47, 48
Beatles' songs
    All I've Got To Do   57
    Can't Buy Me Love   56, 57
    Hold Me Tight   56 58
    She Loves You   58
    Ticket to Ride   113–14
    Yes It Is   114–16
BEETHOVEN   15
    Seventh Symphony   14, 34, 68
Ben Hur, music for   119
BERLIN, IRVING   103
BERNSTEIN, L., *West Side Story*   126
BILK, ACKER   25, 119

Bits and Pieces, Dave Clark Five   55,
    76–77
BLESH, RUDI, *Shining Trumpets*   40,
    43
Blues   24, 39–40, 54, 56, 57
Boheme, La   3
BRAHMS   67
BRAUN, M., *The Beatles' Progress*   75
BROWN, J. A. C., *Techniques of
    Persuasion*   67, 69, 77
BRUBECK, DAVE   25, 43, 62, 121, 125
BULL, JOHN, *Walsingham*   10
BURNEY, DR., music as an innocent
    luxury   15

CARLYLE   90
CHARLES, RAY   125
Charts of pop music   73
Children's remarks about music
    106–110
Church music   9–10
Cinema, popular culture in   48
Classical Period   13–18
Club pianist   50
C.N.D. songs   101
COGAN, ALMA   48–49
Concert, effect on teenagers   72–73
Concert favourites   96
Concert halls, building of   15
Concert programmes in the nine-
    teenth century   16
Contemporary composers   96
COOKE, DERYCK   85, *The Language
    of Music*   2
Coon   18
COPLAND, A.
    Clarinet Concerto   126
    Dance Symphony   122

135